PUBLISHED BY ROBERT CORBIN

COUPLE POWER

Published By Robert Corbin

@ Tami Collins

Couple Power: Reach Your Best Version Discovering the

Synergie With the Love of Your Life

All Right RESERVED

ISBN 978-87-94477-90-1

TABLE OF CONTENTS

Chapter 1 1

Develop Deep Personal Interest 1

Chapter 2 4

Endearing Words Will Get You Far 4

Chapter 3 10

Power Up Positivity In Partnership 10

Chapter 4 16

Working Together 16

Chapter 5 23

Power Of Dreams 23

Chapter 6 26

Finding Time For Self-Care 26

Chapter 7 37

High-Performance Mindset 37

Chapter 9 65

Beginnings Of A Legend 65

Chapter 10 68

Love Is… 68

Chapter 11 73

Cultivating Intimacy 73

Chapter 12 75

Power Of Love 75

Chapter13 80

Strategies For Managing Stress And Fatigue 80

Chapter 14 95

Time Management 95

Chapter 15 107

Power Of Faith 107

Chapter 16 110

Reath & Meditation 110

Chapter 1

Develop Deep Personal Interest

Here's something to ponder on. Why is it that in the first few weeks of dating, you can remember every single detail of what your lover says?

You remember dates, details, emotions, and other things; however, months later, you are unable to keep up. You forget dates; details are now a bore, and emotional issues are now dramatic in your opinion. What changed?

Did the individual suddenly become less fun, less attractive, or less of what you want? Truthfully speaking, human nature is selfish, and you can only show complete interest in another person for so long before you revert to focusing on the number one person—yourself. Here's something to practice with your lover. Write out ten questions about yourself and have them write out ten questions about themselves. Exchange the question papers and try to answer them.

You may realize that you both either do not know enough about yourselves or are unable to retain certain information about yourselves no matter how many times it has been repeated. Don't feel guilty or distressed about this. Trust me, very few get it right the first time. The issue is that most people date without a deep-rooted interest in their counterparts. Try these questions and marvel at what answers you might get:

- Who is my best friend?

- What's my favorite show or movie?

- Where did I grow up?

- What did I study in school?

- How old am i?

- What is the nature of my job?

- What's my last name?

- What's my favorite meal?

- What did I wear yesterday?

- What are my short-term and long-term goals?

Let's face it; your lover may not be able to answer many of these questions. It would stand as an eye-opener and would point them in the right direction, and thereafter there should be an improvement in the details that they retain.

When you develop a deep personal interest with your partner, you tend to pick up on little personal information and in some cases, you act as a "sticky note" for them, even when they forget certain things about their own lives.

Have you ever had your lover call you up to remind you of a business appointment, or some other thing that you forgot without having a stake or personal gain in that particular event? If you are yet to try it, that's how you practice being a very important aspect of a person's life.

In some cases, you may not be dating the person officially, but I guarantee that if you took interest in their personal affairs to the level of dedicating time to listen to them, push them to improve themselves, and you take selfless interest in their life activities, they would inadvertently reciprocate, and you both would find yourselves in a stronger friendship than ever before.

This isn't left to a specific gender; both genders can take up this challenge. This may be more difficult for females but come naturally to males because males are hunters, and females mostly play the role of attracting the males and playing hard to get for as long as possible.

To the women, I say this: when you have discovered the man that you would like to give access to, and you find him worthy of you, the best way to ensure that you both stand the test of time and eventually take things to the next level is by showing that much interest in his personal life even without his wanting to discuss it.

This would score you far ahead of every other female lurking around in his life, both past and present.

Chapter 2

Endearing Words Will Get You Far

Good old-fashioned "sugar tongue" is one of the traditions that is fast phasing out. The modern use of endearing words is grossly limited to the generic ones that are widely used everywhere. It's completely boring.

So, here's what I mean. I had a friend of mine who was a bit of a wildcard and loved adventure, go to a shopping mall to carry out an experiment.

He stood at a place where there were a couple of females around and he said the word "baby." Over 70% of the female population turned to look at him.

It showed the commonness of this word. We tried another name in the same manner. He stood at a strategic place and he said "harlequin." Both males and females turned around to see who he could be referring to.

The inference is that endearing words have to be unique to be really appreciated. It is proven that many people that have peculiar endearing names stay longer in that relationship even when it has become too toxic for comfort.

These names often have a stronghold on the individual and are often used to calm anger and other negative emotions even faster than the generic ones such as "baby" which literally holds little to no value today.

You do not have to be a creative genius to come up with endearing names and words, simple appreciation for doing absolutely nothing can be quite pleasing.

In another light, using fun, animals' names can often do the trick when used right. For example cuddle bunny, bean bug, big teddy, cute kitten, and others. When is the right time to use endearing words? Every single time!

You do not have to wait for a special occasion to smoothly slide these names into conversations. Do NOT only use them when you need favors or else the aim is defeated.

Forgive Completely

So, I was invited to a couple's counseling session, and I was opportune, as a witness, to experience the intensity of the hot vocal exchanges that blared across the room between two individuals who were in a serious relationship but decided to go for counseling before calling it quits if counseling should fail of course.

You could tell that forgiveness is a rare gift that only very few possessed when you listen to various people talk about the things that they disliked about their lovers.

You will always hear of misdoings and mistakes made in the near-past and very distant past that the perpetrator may have apologized for on various occasions, but somehow these issues remained fresh in memory and always come back, and still stand as a major barrier to why couples cannot move on.

Why is it easier to forget all the good times, and the good and selfless deeds but easier to remember the hurt, the bad memories, and even petty arguments that make absolutely no sense? This was clearly a clog in the way of progress but it is never easy to just forget.

How then can we make our lovers forget about the unpleasant past and retain more of the satisfying memories? The truth is that there is no silver bullet to this.

It is an individual strength and or weakness. The strongest of us all is that person who is able to forgive wrong and bury its memories, freeing themselves of its shackling negative emotion and unhappiness.

Those of us will have weaker emotions and will struggle with the intensity of this negative memory and it fights us every time we try to move on. You have to understand something; you may have forgiven your lover for a certain misdeed and have decided to move on, but the memory will remain and haunt you because of the gap in emotional strength.

The person who committed the act is clear of the sin, but you still hold an undying grudge that lodges in your system like a virus, multiplying and eating away at your sanity, happiness, and capacity to operate freely as before.

If we are not able to forgive others, even in our own imperfections, we are unworthy of any type of forgiveness by any person for that matter.

Those people that grow into admirable couples, and are envied by all because of their closeness and understanding of each other, are usually the ones with the greater challenges. However, they never show their flaws outside.

They defend each other with their last breath in the eyes of the general public, and then they sit and discuss matters in a civilized and respectful manner in private.

Forgiveness doesn't take away hurt, but it gives the future a chance and solidifies the bond between both parties.

How long should it take you to forgive? What if the problem is critical and deserves a period of time out to reassess and reevaluate before even talking about forgiveness?

These questions are completely understandable, especially in the case of cheating. Cheating is arguably the most critical problem in any relationship, right next to physical abuse.

How does one forgive cheating or even physical abuse, and move on like nothing ever happened? How do you stop such memories from lingering?

These are very important questions to ask yourself because, in the end, it is them that wear the shoes that understand where they pinch.

Forgiveness is a tool that is used to build a solid relationship, but you also have to know when to use this tool and when this tool is not applicable.

There are certain unspoken rules in relationships, for example, if your relationship has experienced physical abuse, it is very unlikely that forgiveness is the best tool to apply.

You must sit with a professional counselor or a close confidant to discuss the causes and effects of this act in detail. Remaining in a relationship where there is physical abuse is highly discouraged.

Now, let's talk about cheating.

There is no excuse for cheating. It's pretty black and white; you wanted to have sexual relations with a person and you did. Some may call it a moment of weakness, and some may say that it was the effect of being neglected in their own relationship, but here's a thought.

If we were all to react according to our weaknesses, would there be a single faithful person on earth? I think not. It's always best to remove yourself from complicated, situations, relationships, friendships, and occasions that might bring out the wild side.

Is cheating forgivable? Yes, it is, absolutely! How long should it take to forgive a partner who cheats on you? in my experience, the time may differ from one person to another, but if you truly love this person and would really like a future with them in it, then I beg of you, do not take too long in stretching the hand of forgiveness.

No one is perfect, and it can happen to the best of us no matter what anyone thinks. Taking too long to forgive a partner who cheated on you can be likened to leaving a child outside the front porch in the snowy weather because he or she was being a nuisance.

The problem with this is that the child will knock and plead for forgiveness as long as they can until the cold starts to hit hard or until a kind stranger outside decides to offer a warm bed and some hot soup.

Trust me on this, whether it is the right decision to make or not, at that time, your partner is extremely vulnerable and can become easily enticed by the slightest show of kindness or empathy from someone else; this of course is dangerous to your relationship.

So, take your time to heal, but make sure that you heal creatively and that your partner understands their wrong deeds and is willing to make amends. If cheating occurs more than once, then you are justified to leave the relationship asap!

Chapter 3

Power Up Positivity in Partnership

In a world enamored with grand gestures, million-dollar weddings, and extravagant declarations of love, it's easy to overlook the quieter, more profound moments that truly make a relationship thrive. While society, with its glitzy portrayal of "perfect" couples, may have us believe that love is measured by the size of a diamond or the number of likes on a romantic post, the Bible offers a different perspective. "Above all, love each other deeply, because love covers over a multitude of sins.

Powering up in a relationship doesn't necessarily mean a high-profile presence or a life free from challenges. Instead, it refers to fostering a partnership where positivity reigns supreme, where hope is the bedrock, and where both individuals lift each other up, especially during the storms of life. It's about cultivating an environment where faith takes precedence over fear, and where the shared vision is rooted in Christ's teachings.

In this chapter, we will delve deep into the Christian perspective on infusing relationships with genuine positivity. Through biblical teachings, real-life examples, and actionable insights, we aim to unravel the true essence of a God-centered partnership that radiates joy, understanding, and unwavering faith.

No relationship, not even those of our favorite celebrities, is immune to challenges. However, it's the perspective with which we approach these challenges that makes all the difference. As we journey through "Power Up," let's embrace the lessons and the blessings that come from placing God at the center of our love stories, ensuring that the partnership thrives on genuine positivity and profound spiritual connection.

The Language of Hope in Relationships

One of the most powerful tools in a relationship is communication, and within that vast realm of interaction lies a subset so potent yet so understated: the language of hope. This unique language goes beyond mere words; it's a harmonious blend of verbal affirmations, actions, and an inherent belief in the potential and future of the partnership. It serves as an anchor, grounding the relationship in optimism even when the waters get tumultuous.

Relationships, like ships, require steady anchors to prevent them from drifting amidst the unpredictable currents of life. One of the most potent anchors for a relationship is a shared vision of the future. When couples craft and commit to a shared future, they not only foster unity and purpose but also provide stability and direction for their relationship. Here's how future plans serve as relationship anchors:

Shared Goals and Vision: Discussing and designing a shared future provides clarity about the couple's collective aspirations. Whether it's purchasing a home, planning vacations, setting career objectives, or deciding on family expansion, these shared goals unify the couple, providing a roadmap to navigate life's journey together.

Promotes Commitment: The act of setting future plans underscores the couple's commitment to each other. When you talk about and invest in your shared future, it reinforces the idea that both partners are in it for the long haul.

Acts as a Safety Net: Life is fraught with challenges, and disagreements within relationships are inevitable. However, having established future plans can serve as a constant reminder of the bigger picture and the couple's mutual intentions, helping them to work through tough times and conflicts.

Fosters Communication: Planning for the future requires open and consistent communication. Through discussions about future aspirations, dreams, and concerns, couples strengthen their communication skills, learning to express desires, fears, and expectations clearly.

Encourages Growth: Shared future plans can motivate individual and collective growth. They push both partners to be better, not just for themselves, but for the sake of the partnership. This can lead to personal development, skill acquisition, and emotional maturity.

Strengthens Bonding: Engaging in future planning activities, whether it's creating a financial plan, attending pre-marital or relationship growth classes, or even house hunting, can be bonding experiences. They provide opportunities for couples to make memories, learn more about each other, and solidify their union.

Keeps Priorities in Check: When both partners have a clear understanding of their future plans, it's easier to prioritize daily actions and decisions that align with those plans. This can prevent distractions and deviations that might pull the relationship off course.

Reinforces Faith and Trust: For Christian couples, future plans also involve entrusting their shared journey to God. Proverbs 16:9 says, "In their hearts humans plan their course, but the Lord establishes their steps." While planning, it's essential to also seek divine guidance and maintain faith that God will lead the way.

Future plans, when crafted thoughtfully and pursued with commitment, act as formidable anchors that keep relationships stable and centered. They remind couples of their shared purpose, fortifying their bonds against the storms they might face together.

Staying positive and hopeful in a relationship, particularly during turbulent times, requires a shared effort and commitment to growth and understanding. Here are some practical ways to foster optimism and hopefulness within a romantic relationship:

Open Communication: Regularly talk to each other about feelings, expectations, and concerns. Honest and open dialogue can build trust and prevent misunderstandings.

Express Appreciation: Regularly expressing gratitude and appreciation for each other fosters positivity. Compliment each other, say thank you, and acknowledge each other's efforts and contributions.

Set Shared Goals Future planning and setting shared goals can anchor a relationship, providing a common vision that you're working towards together. Whether it's saving for a house, planning a vacation, or working on personal growth, having shared goals unites couples.

Spend Quality Time Together: Invest in quality time, not just quantity. Engage in activities that both enjoy, even if it's as simple as a shared meal without distractions.

Maintain Individuality: While togetherness is vital, respecting and nurturing individual spaces and hobbies is equally essential. Encourage each other in personal hobbies and interests.

Seek Professional Help if Needed: Sometimes, having a mediator like a couples therapist can provide guidance tailored to your relationship's specific needs.

Develop a Positivity Ritual: Create rituals or routines that allow you to connect positively, such as a weekly date night or nightly gratitude sharing before bed.

Avoid Blame and Criticism: When conflicts arise, focus on resolving the issue rather than blaming or criticizing each other.

Build a Support System: Engaging with friends or family members who support your relationship can provide an additional positivity layer.

Avoid Unhealthy Comparisons:** Every relationship is unique, and comparing yours to others' can create unnecessary strain. Focus on what works for your relationship.

Work on Trust: Trust is the foundation of any healthy relationship. It must be nurtured and protected. Be trustworthy and give trust.

Have Fun Together: Remember to keep the joy alive. Play, laugh, and enjoy each other's company.

Keep Romance Alive: Regularly engage in romantic gestures, big or small, to keep the spark alive.

Embrace Change Together: Accept that change is inevitable, whether in individual lives or as a couple. Embrace it together, adapt, and grow.

Pray or Meditate Together: If you share spiritual beliefs, engaging in spiritual practices together can deepen your connection.

Learn Each Other's Love Language: Understanding how your partner feels loved and appreciated helps in expressing love in a way that resonates with them.

Cultivate a Shared Vision of Success: Talk openly about what success means for your relationship, be it financial stability, emotional connection, or something else, and work together towards that vision.

Focus on the Positive: Encourage a practice where you both share something positive about each other or your day. This routine can foster a habit of looking for the good.

Encourage Growth and Support Dreams: Be each other's cheerleaders. Encourage personal and professional growth, and support each other's dreams.

Practice Forgiveness: Mistakes happen. Learning to forgive and not holding onto grudges enables healing and growth.

The key to staying positive and hopeful in a relationship is intentional effort and mutual commitment to growth, understanding, love, and respect. Remember, every relationship has its own dynamics, and these guidelines can be tailored to fit what suits you and your partner best.

Chapter 4

WORKING TOGETHER

have a lot of admiration for donkeys and the couple power used to carry the kind of heavy load that they have to carry. Horses use horse power to run their

races. Donkeys use couple power to pull heavily loaded carts. When working together, donkeys must demonstrate oneness, team spirit, selfless consideration to pull carts. In order to accomplish their assigned task, they have to co-ordinate their movements. They must be of one mind and purpose. As long as they are yoked together, they must agree on selfless discipline. Usually, they eat grass from one side first and when this is finished, they move together to eat from another side. They serve no selfish interest whatsoever because any selfish move could be fatal. They even coordinate their steps when walking. This is couple power.

The Bible says in 2 Corinthians 6:14, "Do not be yoked together with unbelievers." Being unequally yoked together can be a daunting task and very scaring because you have nothing in common. Your goals and ambitions are different. As I watch donkeys carrying heavy loads, I feel sorry for them but also wonder why people should beat them so ruthlessly when they faithfully serve them by carrying loads that they themselves cannot bear.

A young donkey being trained for the career of pulling the cart gets yoked together with two older veterans who mentor the young one until the new donkey learns the skill of pulling the cart and coordinating its steps in the same direction. Cooperation in all they do is of essence for their benefit and survival. When the newcomer is considered to have acquired the necessary skills from this mentorship, it is released to be yoked with a different donkey so as to begin the work of pulling the carts as a new couple.

Donkey couples have to agree on a lot of things. They have for example to agree when to walk, to run or to stop - together. They have to agree on which way to go so that the two can go in the same direction without pulling each other in the opposite direction which would result to injury and become counter- productive. If they do not work together, they can easily kill each other. They must therefore have a common purpose in their entire life of their donkey years so long as they are yoked together to exercise couple power.

This was just an illustration of donkey couple power that more intelligent human beings could learn from and adopt as a life style. The important point in this illustration is that couples yoked together must agree to work together in order to avoid among other things emotional hurts. Separation and divorce steal couple power and cause devastating emotional injury until and unless the Lord intervenes. This is why vital lessons could be learned by observing donkeys at work and as they exercise and demonstrate couple power per excellence.

Horse Power

We often hear and read about horse power but hardly do we hear or read about donkey power. I have a water pump that has a 4 horse power. There is so much hype about horses. Throughout the world, horse races normally get a lot of publicity. Many people bet on the winning horse. Horses are also pampered a great deal. They have shoes fitted on their feet and given nutritious feed complete with supplements. Some of them have mind boggling and tongue twisting praise names. They are powerful and very beautiful to look at. Horse lovers will spend money on their horses and will shed tears when their favorite horse dies, just like all animal lovers.

Compared to donkeys, horses are competitors. They work in singles and for them to compete in a horse race, their burden is made light. They run to compete. The horse rider must be experienced in using maneuvers or schemes that outdo and out run the rest of the competitors. They have no idea about using couple power for they cannot be yoked together to run the race. Even the rider cannot be yoked together with the horse. They are simply incompatible. That is why my only vote goes to the donkey because it is a demonstration of couple power per excellence.

We have a big oak tree near our village. It bears edible fruits soon after our Equatorial rains. This tree is very tall. It takes an experienced strong man to carefully climb and shake it enough for the fruits to fall down. As the fruits fall from the tree, they scatter all over the base of the tree. Once the man thinks he has enough fruits for the family, he comes down and leaves his wife to gather the fruits. The wife gathers the fruits carefully and carries them home, prepares them well and finally obeys her motherly instinct to serve her family. I wonder who in this case did the bigger job. Is it the one who shook the tree or the one who gathered the fruits and served the family?

This question never arose in my village. It was assumed all along that the husband climbs and shakes the tree and the wife gathers the fruits for the family. It is a true demonstration of couple power because both husband and wife have achieved what they are suited for individually and have both selflessly accomplished their tasks for the benefit of the family.

Couple power is also like drawing strength from your fingers on your right hand and interlocking them with the other five fingers on your left hand to form a bigger and a more resilient fist. When these ten fingers are interlocked, they have more strength together. Interlocking fingers, however, does not mean that they lose their individual identity. They have not dissolved into each other like two tablets in a glass of water. Each hand keeps its own identity and operates in a way most suited for it. In the same way, the couple simply merges their strengths and their individual gifts and talents for their common good and should remain a merger. A merger is not equivalent to being absorbed into some tasteless liquid. The couple has simply merged their different strengths and talents for their selfless and common good which creates the much needed Couple Power.

Priscilla and Aquila

In the Bible we have many characters but in the book of Acts 18 my attention is drawn to a Jewish couple, Priscilla and Aquila, whom Paul met in Corinth. I particularly admire Priscilla and Aquila who in their service to God showed couple power. Out of the six times the couple is mentioned, Priscilla's name comes first. What surprises me is that Aquila does not seem to be bothered by the fact that his wife is recognized first. This reversed and unusual order of recognizing man and wife does not seem to erode his self-worth as a man or deflate his ego or sense of significance. Note that we do not usually say wife and husband. It even feels quite odd and almost becomes a tongue twister. Aquila is not bothered by what he possibly considers a trivial matter in their marriage journey. They simply show their oneness in their tent making business and in their joint ministry as evangelists in the church which was being held at their home. They enjoyed exercising their couple power regardless of who was recognized or received credit for the work done by both of them.

It is strange that sometimes spouses become jealous of each other especially where one person feels that credit is going to the wrong person who least deserves it. This was not a matter of concern for Priscilla and Aquila. They are such a great example of a couple that you cannot help admiring their maturity in demonstrating couple power in action because they do not suffer from petty jealousies between them. This indeed is a couple that has mentored all of us. In modern day language we would say that their password in life is together and their username is couple power.

How I have benefited.

Esther, one of our young ladies in the church was planning to have a wedding. As older women in the church, we decided to come together to help in the planning. Initially we thought that the meeting was going to be a ladies only meeting to discuss our role in the upcoming Esther's wedding. However, after a second thought and as the Lord would have it, the Holy Spirit prompted me to call the other two ladies and asked them to kindly bring along their spouses. My friends quickly organized for a couples meeting and within an hour or so, they had brought their spouses with them for some kind of unplanned fellowship/dinner.

My hubby was already home and I wanted him to enjoy the fellowship and to participate in the discussion in the company of his friends and also with the other men. Most importantly, I wanted him to give me the necessary cover and to help me in chairing and facilitating the meeting. I needed all his support because I knew that I enjoyed free style fellowships and discussions rather than the formal meetings which I was meant to facilitate that evening. It is for these two reasons that I suddenly felt that the other two male spouses needed to participate in the fellowship and in the discussions. Their participatory input was quite invaluable. This kind of arrangement was beneficial for everyone because we all enjoyed the fellowship, spirited discussion and contribution to the agenda before us. It worked out much better than how we had initially planned it, to have men wait at home, instead of involving them directly.

In short, the meeting went on very well and couples sat in pairs to fully exercise their couple power. This was necessary because we had a chance to correct and appraise each other during our discussion that evening. Seated this way, spouses could use private codes to prompt each other or approve each other accordingly. As usual, James used our familiar code. My good hubby gently steps on my toes to communicate as he did in this case. This signal quickly tells me that I have gone overboard and should be careful.

James, unlike me ends his day around 9 o'clock at night while mine lingers on much longer. When the meeting went on far too long, his body clock and internal alarm clock rung, he dozed off leaving all worldly cares behind and signaling loud and clear to me that I had temporarily lost my cover and veteran prompter. Taking this loud cue, I therefore concluded the meeting rather hurriedly but thanked God for a fruitful discussion and fellowship which was powered by God given couple power.

This case portrays couple power and the need to cover for each other in good and in bad times till death do us part. I am aware that we are created different and that couples have to deal with unmet expectations in marriage. This initial disappointment on couple expectations could make some unwise couples conclude that they have irreconcilable differences leading to incompatibility in marriage. Wise couples, however, will see their differences as strengths with which to work for the benefit of their marriage and family.

Once you appreciate that your spouse is made differently from you, one can begin to view them as designer made and appreciate the fact that they passed the designer's quality check with a grade A on average.

We all need to remember that, after the creation of man and woman, the Lord was so pleased with what he had personally designed and created, and (including your spouse) that He pronounced and confirmed that his finished masterpiece was very good. After this superb design, there was nothing else he needed to add or subtract to improve on his creation and design and so he rested on the seventh day after an excellent and awesome job well done.

You and I are the only ones who waste precious time and opportunity thinking that God's work of design and creation of your spouse and mine is incomplete while God finished with them a long time ago. Strange as it sounds, you as couples could be wasting precious time with wishful thinking and chasing after the wind by trying to improve on your spouse who is already a well finished product with a unique personality.

Chapter 5

Power of Dreams

Define your dream.

How do you define a dream? A dream is something that you wish and hope for since you were a kid. A lot of people dream of owning a big house, a nice car, and lots of money. Others dream of becoming a professional, like a doctor, lawyer, accountant, and engineer, or inherit the family business. Some would like to travel the world with their loved ones, or get married and have their own kids, raising them to be good Christians and citizens. We all dream. There is no exception to it. We may differ in the intensity and feeling of our dreams but these dreams motivate us to work hard and overcome challenges in life.

We both love to be of service to other people. We use our God-given talents especially in communication to help them achieve their own dreams. One of our friends and mentor, book-writing coach Sha Nacino inspired us to write our purpose statement. Through her Mission Happiness conference, we learned the value of knowing your purpose in life. She said that when you are clear with your WHY, then every decision you make will be anchored in it. Whenever opportunities come your way, it would be easier for you to say YES or NO.

Everyone has ambitions in life.

When you were a child, you would often have people ask you: "What would you like to be when you grow up?" You would just say anything that comes to mind. But as you grow older, you notice that your answers become different. These are influenced by a lot of factors: the environment, the people you are with, the shows that you watched, your mentors, and the different opportunities and challenges that may come your way. Nevertheless, we must remain to be vigilant in our ambitions. Always aim for the best in your life and in the lives of other people surrounding you.

Napoleon Hill said, in his book Think and Grow Richtruly, thoughts are things and powerful things at that, when they are mixed with definiteness of purpose, persistence, and a BURNING DESIRE for their translation into riches, or other material objects."

What drives you? Does your dream fuel you to give your best every day? Successful people would recommend that you dream BHAG. B stands for BIG, H is for Hairy, A for Audacious and G for Goal. Dreams are so big that it can overwhelm you. When this happens, you are inspired to take BIG actions towards attaining your goals.

People would often wish that God grant the desires of their heart. What does that really mean? It is not just the dreams that you have but also the feelings that drive you to reach for those goals. Are the feelings intense enough that it will make you move? What do you want to feel when you achieve those dreams? We all want to be loved right? We all want to feel that we are enough and that we are worthy.

How do you make one?

- Make a list of your dreams by writing down at least one goal for each area of your life. It has to be clear and specific.

- Once you have finished with your list, start finding pictures which best represent your goals. It can be cut from newspapers or magazines or printed from images in the internet.
- Arrange those pictures on a board and place it in an area of your house or room where you will always be reminded of your goals. It doesn't matter if you are not artistically inclined. What is important is placing what you really want on your vision board.

Chapter 6

Finding Time for Self-Care

Eing a parent is a full-time job that never stops, and it can be easy to lose sight of your own needs and well-being while juggling work, family, and other responsibilities. However, taking care of yourself is crucial to being the best parent you can be. Finding time for yourself and for self-care is not only beneficial for your own mental and physical health, but it can also improve your relationships with your children and partner. As a dad, a mom or partner, it's important to prioritize self-care and make time for it in your daily routine. This can be challenging, but with the right strategies and mindset, it is possible to find a healthy balance between parenting and taking care of yourself.

Between the number of things to do each day, the daily routine and the desire to want to take care of others, when should you take time for yourself when you are a parent? We run to the right to take the children to the sport. You run till the wheels come off to do the shopping for the week. When you have a little time without anything planned, you take the opportunity to tidy up the house or do your kids' school paperwork. You don't really take time for yourself anymore. You feel tense, stressed and vulnerable, and the first people that get the short end of the stick are your loved ones. By wanting to do too much, you completely forget yourself. But being a good parent, it also means taking care of yourself as you do your kids. The theme for this week, month, or even year is simple yet so important: make time for yourself. As a parent, it's easy to get caught up in the endless chores and activities that come with caring for our little ones (who, let's face it, aren't always as cute as we'd like them to be). Before we know it, months or even years have gone by and we realize we've forgotten to take care of ourselves. So today, we're not going to be talking about children, we're going to be talking about YOU, me, us adults, and our needs.

- Take Time for Yourself When You Are a Mom / Dad: More Ideas
- "A day for yourself" with Warren Andrews
- So take a few minutes for yourself right now, starting by reading the following to improve your well-being without feeling guilty.
- Why Take Time For Yourself?
- Take Care of Yourself to Better Take Care of Others
- Take Breaks to Avoid Burnout
- How Do You Take Time For Yourself?
- How to Take Time for Yourself When You Are Parents without Feeling Guilty?

Why Take Time For Yourself?

Taking time for yourself is giving yourself importance! We don't have to choose between the development of your children and the prosperity of your own. Doing both is achievable. Moreover, the two are linked since if you have time to take care of yourself, you become more fulfilled to take care of your children.

Because taking time for yourself is taking care of yourself : having time for yourself is choosing what you really want to do for yourself, to pamper yourself, to fulfill yourself, to indulge in a passion and to exercise.

Because it's about making choices. To choose something is to give up something else. Taking time for yourself also means choosing to place yourself in front of your own responsibilities, and realizing that you are responsible for what you are, what you do and who you become. Having to make choices pushes us to clearly set our priorities (and not just to follow the course of things because the machine is carried away and we are running after).

Because we need to realize ourselves. We're not just a mom,dad or partner. One is not only the spouse of. We are not just the employee or the boss. We are not only the parent who manages the learning of the children. We all earned our parental badges, but at some point we also have the right to take them off, to be as just ourselves, with all of our desires, needs, projects, dreams, aspirations, challenges and passions.

Because we need rest. It is vital for our physical, mental, psychological and emotional health.

Take Care of Yourself to Better Take Care of Others

I recently got my first aid training booster for work. One of the first things we are taught is that before stepping in to help an injured person, you must first protect yourself. The trainers always insist on this point by saying that a dead or injured rescuer will be of no use to the victim, and it's so true

It's the same principle when you fly; the safety instruction is to put the oxygen mask on yourself first before putting it on your child. Quite simply because if you fall unconscious, you will not be able to help your child. It's quite easy to understand but not always easy to apply. Instinct, especially in parents, is more often to take care of others before taking care of ourselves. And yet taking time for yourself when you're parents is not an option, it's a duty.

Take Breaks to Avoid Burnout

We tend to try to fill each of our free moments with a "useful" activity in order to feel productive. But if you pull too much on the rope, it may end up snapping. This is the moment when you will feel exhausted even if you did nothing all day long. You will be irritable, tired. Your relationships with others will be strained. You may want to send everything flying. Why? Because you are exhausted!

On a daily basis, your energy is spent but never recharged. It's like a battery, when it has lost all its energy; it is no longer of any use. Either throw it away or reload it. Of course, I advise you to recharge your internal batteries before they are completely flat. I don't know about you, but when I try to do too many things at the same time, I do them wrong and in the end I waste more time, because I have to redo them. So what if we tried to do less but better and above all to take breaks and recharge our batteries and finally take some time for ourselves?

At first, you can feel guilty about taking care of yourself. But then, you stop feeling guilty. I highly recommend usings a sleep tracker. You make think you are getting enough sleep but you may find out quickly that you are falling significantly short of healthy thresholds.

How Do You Take Time For Yourself?

Taking time for yourself as a parent can feel like a luxury or even a guilty pleasure, but it is essential for your mental, emotional, and physical well-being. There is no magic method. There are habits to adopt, systems to simplify, choices to make too. And all of this will evolve over the months and years, as your children grow and gain autonomy.

Here are plenty of avenues to explore:

Organize and simplify storage at home and teach your children from an early age to tidy up.

Do a little each day: spread household chores over the week.

Everyone participates in life at home (to the extent of their abilities), even the children.

Save time in the kitchen: cook in larger quantities and freeze your favorite raw recipes that are quick to make and prepare your menus in advance.

Eliminate non-essential activities like ironing.

Teach your children to be independent in their learning.

Have your children looked after from time to time: by the other parent, by the grandparents, by an aunt or uncle, by a friend who has children too or by a neighbor with whom you can alternate and exchange good practices, by a babysitter or a nanny (even once a week if possible).

Go to bed a little later from time to time and make an appointment with yourself.

Or get up earlier without breaking a sleep cycle in the middle.

Don't turn on the TV for two nights a week.

Go a full day without technology: no social media, no phone (except calls and texts), no emails and no video games. Set an activity timer on your phone with lock out. Give the password to your partner

Take time for yourself during a nap: even if the children are not sleeping, they can have a quiet and a nice time without it feeling like a chore.

Play with your children, which will then allow them to play without you around in the future because they will have filled up emotionally. And you will be able to have time for yourself while they are on their own.

Perhaps you tell yourself that among these ideas there are some that are frankly inaccessible. Maybe. Or maybe not that much. Let's say that several elements must be taken into account:

Your fatigue level:

it is real and if you are exhausted, it is true that going to bed later is clearly not a good idea. But there are solutions and I'm living proof. On top of a full time job I ensure I have more than 12 to 15 hours a week to work on writing this book and do things for Me.

The age of your children:

you have to accept the seasons. The toddler season is time-consuming. The little babies need a lot more attention and care than the bigger ones. So you shouldn't try to have as much time for yourself if you have a 6-month-old baby as another parent who has a 6-year-old child. But there are still things to put in place to have a little time for them and increase it as your child grows.

Making choices:

You won't be able to have time for yourself if you don't clearly decide that it's a priority. So you have to be ready to give up other things that will cost you a little now, but will bring you a lot more later on.

How to Take Time for Yourself When You Are Parents without Feeling Guilty?

You are the person you spend 100% of your time with. And yet, I'm sure you don't even spend 80% of your day doing something just for yourself. The percentage isn't really that important, but it's worth taking a day (or rather a week) back to yourself and wondering how much time you actually gave yourself. Try doing the exercise to really be present and self conscious.

As you read in the previous point, to take good care of others, you must first take care of yourself. So, as a parent, if your desire is to take care of your children as well as possible, you must take care of yourself. If you are fulfilled, in good shape and mentally healthy, your children (and your spouse) will benefit from it as much as you will. Do you think your child would prefer a tired, nervous mom, dad or partner with a perfectly clean and tidy house, or a cheerful and smiling parent with a basket of laundry still full and questionable smudges on the wall?

Taking time for yourself when you are a parent is a benevolent act towards yourself but also towards others. So out with the guilt! You are not selfish when you take time for yourself! Quite the contrary!

Make time for yourself despite fear of judgment from others

The judgment of others can be difficult to bear when we feel judged in our role as a parent. Everyone makes their own commentary by criticizing the way others do things. If parent gives the impression of having personal activities, some will think that he must not be a good parent, devoted to his children.

But the important thing is to ask yourself is what is more important to you: to give the impression of being a perfect parent or to be a perfect parent? In any case, others only have access to a small visible part of you. Moreover, they will make THEIR interpretation and will see what they want to see in relation to THEIR system of thoughts. What they think does not define who you are!

To better understand that our thoughts are not universal, I recommend that you read more books on how thoughts influence our reality.

Take time for yourself when you are overwhelmed

I admit, taking time for yourself when you're parents is not always easy, but it's all a matter of priorities. Ask yourself what do you want to give the most importance to at this moment. It is possible that from day to day, your priorities will not be the same. One day you will need more time for yourself, while another day you will feel less need for it. Listen to yourself, because only you will know what you need.

If you think you have a lot to do, consider getting organized. Set priorities and plan your actions. Also consider grouping similar tasks together to save time.

Know how to delegate; you are not alone in knowing how to do things. Everyone can participate. Ask your children to set the table, even if they complain at first. Everyone can store their own laundry. Your husband/wife can take care of certain papers or go shopping. When those around you understand that by helping, they benefit from it because you have more quality time to give them that will motivate them. They are even likely to take the initiative themselves to help or take responsibility for a task.

Sometimes you have to know how to say no! It's very weird at first; you don't really feel comfortable, especially when it's your child who comes to ask you for something. But saying no doesn't mean you're snubbing him. It is quite possible to make your child understand that for the moment, you cannot and you do not have time, or that you need a moment for yourself, and that you will be more available a little later.

Eventually, you will have to accept that not everything will be done or be perfect. And I'll tell you a secret, it doesn't matter!! Your world will still keep spinning.

Take Time for Yourself When You Are a Mom / Dad: More Ideas

Everyone will have their own thing, but here is a small non-exhaustive list to get you started:

- Get a massage or a facial treatment
- Read a book
- Meditate
- Write
- Paint or knit
- Go eat out at a restaurant or have a night out with friends
- Shopping, alone or with company
- Exercise
- Golf
- Learn to play a musical instrument or a new language (Highly recommend Babbel)

Ask yourself what gives you pleasure, what makes you disconnect from everyday life and do it.

Find the thing that excites you and take the time to do it.

"A day for yourself" with Warren Andrews

For my part, I like to write and read books that enrich my creativity and business tool kit. I like these activities because they distract me and keep me entertained! I also often have friends over, post-kid bed time, to enjoy wine and good company.

I also like to do some introspection, to get to know myself better, to see deep within me blockages and beliefs. I heavily rely upon available resources to guide me through exercises.

Some examples would be:

Sit back, close your eyes, relax and breathe deeply. Then visualize yourself at the edge of a river. The place is bathed in a white or blue light.

Visualize a boat sailing towards you. Reliable and robust, it is sent to you for relief. Watch it in detail before leaving the dock near you.

Think about what concerns you most (small or big problems). They can take the form of objects, images, or feelings ...Drop them into the boat and feel relieved.

Observe the boat full of your worries drifting away and feel the lightness it gives you. Follow it with your eyes until it disappears. Come back to reality again now and do so gradually.

Make peace with your five fingers

Touch your thumb with your index finger and remember a time when you felt great physical fatigue.

Touch your thumb to your middle finger and remember a very loving exchange (chat, email, SMS) with a particular person (your lover, your child, or friend).

Touch your thumb to your ring and remember the most affectionate gesture you received. Relive the scene as a gift.

Touch your thumb to your little finger, and think of yourself as if you're in a beautiful dream. Soak deeply in its beauty.

Another concept worth noting is call "Overflows".

You will need a large notebook and to set your alarm clock every morning twenty minutes before the sunrise.

For twenty minutes, write down whatever comes to your mind, without sorting.

Do not worry neither about the style nor the calligraphy. Smaller hassles, major projects. Do not refuse anything, and do not judge anyone.

After the twenty minutes elapse, close the book without reading you.

The purpose of this practice is that you will be relieved of the life you have planned for the life that awaits you. You can read it two months later to take a step back if you need to.

Chapter 7

High-Performance
Mindset

Have you ever hit a crossroads in your life, that pivotal moment where the next decision you make will change your life forever?

I remember sitting yoga style on the floor of my cold, dark, bedroom, one night 13 years ago, alone, just my head buried in my hands, sobbing uncontrollably, saying to myself, this is it, I have hit my moment right now.

I was going through a divorce, my son was in danger by me not having full custody, I had filed for bankruptcy, lost my house which was being auctioned off the next day, and on top of it all I was being harassed 24/7!

As I sat there, I contemplated for the first time in my life what it would be like if I gave up, if I gave in, if I shut down my business and decided to just bag groceries for the rest of my life and not go after my vision and dreams. What if I just took the easy way out!

Everything seemed to be going against me and the stakes were that much higher but when I look back, it was all going perfectly as planned. In that moment, I decided that there was something bigger at stake--- it was my son's safety and our future, it was my vision of being successful and providing for not only my son but my future family that I envisioned down the road.

I made the decision right then and there that I would fight! I would create the life I envisioned because if I took the alternate path, the dark side would prevail and I would have given up on not only my life, but my future family and my son's life. There was no way in hell I was going to do that!

To succeed, I had to change my mindset. I had to reprogram my perspective on life.

Soon after I initiated this mindset change, I met my wife Kristina and over the next couple of years I fought for and won sole physical and legal custody of my son. In the more than a decade that I have been together with my wife, we have three beautiful children, have built thriving businesses, in addition to authoring multiple books.

If I had chosen the easier path of least resistance, nothing that is in my present life would be here, my family wouldn't exist, nor would anything that we accomplished together!!

Really think about this for a moment and the ABSOLUTE POWER in that decision!

I ask you, WHAT WAS YOUR MOMENT or is that moment RIGHT NOW?

You can study personal development all you want, you can go attend Tony Robbins seminars all you want, but when the shit hits the fan, where do the teachings go in most people?

Right out the window!

People typically fall back on their old patterns and they argue their right to fail.

By contrast, high performance people apply the personal development teachings daily no matter what, not just when life throws them curveballs.

They aren't distracted by the external noise and stimuli. They have learned to focus.

They are constantly making small tweaks, tiny adjustments, to keep their focus sharp on their goals. High performance people know the only thing they can control is themselves. Their mindset and discipline and consistency make the difference.

Having a high-performance mindset is where we start on the road to achieving a sustainable and magnificent success.

Create Your Own Avatar

When Hugh Hefner started Playboy magazine, he was an introvert, a shy, unassuming and quiet guy. At some point, he realized that for this business to take off, he needed to be the playboy and live the lifestyle he was writing about.

He was inspired by 007, James Bond and that's when he developed his own character, his own avatar. He dressed a certain way, drove certain flashy cars, became a lady's man and lived a life that most guys aspired too. His entire business empire took off when he got out front with this avatar he created.

A lot of successful people do that. The singer Elton John was struggling early in his career and asked someone in a bar how to become great. The guy advised him, "You have to kill the person you were born to be in order to become the person you want to be." That inspired the struggling singer to get rid of the old avatar, as Hefner had done, by changing his name to Elton John and creating a flamboyant character around that name. The rest is musical history.

You too, need to dispense with your old avatar if it doesn't serve you, and create a new one tailored to your high-performance success.

A star is born when you choose the self you want to be.

To create that new avatar, start by finding people who possess the attributes you want. If you want to be a great communicator, find the best communicator. If you want to dress a certain way, find someone to model for that. Find people who are what you want to become and take pieces from each of them.

At first you may copy but then you begin to slowly form your own identity. Most people who seem to be original actually borrowed from others and modeled themselves after what they admired in others.

I've had a lot of mentors, starting with my father. I loved Richard Branson, for example, admiring how resourceful, action oriented and limitless he is. I had a multi-billionaire mentor named Errol(RIP), who inspired me by following the principles laid out in the Napoleon Hill book, Think and Grow Rich. Dallas Mavericks owner Mark Cuban is another inspiring example for me and I modeled my focus practice from him.

Find your own mentors, choose them wisely, so your new avatar persona and high-performance mindset effectively and consistently follows your blueprint for success.

Listen to Internal GPS Wisdom

Right after graduating from high school, I was supposed to go to St Anselm's College in New Hampshire and then, mid-summer, my gut said NO. I called them and politely said that I wouldn't be attending their school in September. Instead, I did a 180-degree turn and applied to the University of Wyoming, which was 2,600 miles from my little hometown in Massachusetts, and the rest is ... well, the rest is me!

My decision made no logical sense at the time and more than a few people thought I was acting crazy. I actually didn't know too much about the school – I just knew I had to go there. But it was the best choice I could have made because it came from my heart and soul.

That decision catapulted me to where I am right now at this moment. I grew from an extremely shy, little, eighteen-year-old boy into the man I would become during my four years there.

Yes, listening to your gut is important. It's part of acknowledging your self-worth to realize that you are worth listening to, whatever anyone else is saying.

It sends us messages in several different ways, including uncertainty, hesitation, nagging feelings, curiosity, doubt, gut feelings, suspicion and, most powerful of all, fear.

If you get the feeling that something just isn't right, it probably isn't. Equally, if you get the feeling that you should go for something, even if it doesn't make logical sense, then you should! You need to learn to trust yourself by trusting your intuition because it's like a built-in navigation system, leading to where you are supposed to be in life at a specific moment in time.

Just think of the Kevin Costner movie, Field of Dreams. In the film, Costner's character started hearing a voice saying, 'If you build it, he will come.' What did he build? A baseball field, and he had to tear out rows of corn on his farm to do it. This made no logical sense to him, his family or others in the community. But he followed his intuition and extraordinary things started to happen as a result.

We all possess that voice of wise counsel and guidance inside of us, but sometimes it's communicating so softly you don't listen to it or you choose to discount it as unimportant. Believe me, that's a BIG mistake!

Intuition is a huge tool in sensing and creating opportunities. I am a spontaneous person who listens to my heart and soul. I go with my feelings. It's so easy to overthink things. I went with my gut on changing colleges, changing internships, moving into our dream home. I pulled an offer on a house because it didn't feel right.

It's like a voice telling me when something isn't right. I've used it so much its accurate 99 percent of the time. Intuition is important to a high-performance life. It's a power to sense and act on opportunities. Go with the flow and don't question everything so much.

If you overthink things you can fuck yourself over. Do you have an awareness of an internal voice? When does it come up for you?

If you start listening to that voice, it becomes a habit. In the beginning it's uncomfortable but like building that avatar the discomfort will go away if you keep it up. Don't stop because of fear. Listen to that voice you've been burying in all of the mind noise.

Thinkers are so used to logic they usually don't practice going with their gut. That's foreign to them and using it will make them uncomfortable, but growth comes with that discomfort. It opens doors and helps push the envelope to expand perceived limits.

When you open those perception doors, magical things begin to happen. On my early morning drives to work, when I lived in Massachusetts, I did affirmations (a powerful ritual I describe later in this chapter.) On one of these drives I began thinking about laser focus, and literally as I was thinking this, at four thirty in the morning, a car pulled in front of me and its license plate said focus.

Another time I was thinking about the word quantum and again, a car pulled in front of me with a license plate that said quantum. Both of these synchronistic experiences occurred at four thirty in the morning with few cars on the road. What are the odds of that?

I was just learning at that time about the word synchronicity---meaningful patterns of coincidences. Those experiences lit another fire under me. The power of intention, framing the right mindset, listening to my intuition and being aware of the signs that I was on the right path, these shifts literally marked when the game changed for me. The money flowed for us it was like a waterfall.

Napoleon Hill of Think and Grow Rich fame was right! My wife and I haven't looked back. We are living proof that persistence, combined with high performance mindset and openness to the voice of intuition, truly pays off in joyous and unexpected ways.

Identify & Subjugate Limiting Beliefs

Lots of information gets presented to us through our senses; it all goes into our brain where it is processed and a belief is created. Your brain truly doesn't know the difference between a real and imagined experience. All your brain has to refer to when it comes to making decisions about anything is the information that it receives. It's what you do inside your brain that really matters.

Let's use my wife as a real-life example. She's had a fear of public speaking since college because of one bad experience. She would still talk about how much she hated speaking in front of large groups of people many years later. The information in her mind was that she gave a talk in front of some other students and it didn't go well. What came next were the feelings and emotions that the brain releases.

Let's say you process the information and tell yourself that it was bad, scary and nerve-wracking as most people would. When you've processed the event you've experienced, you start to feel the associated emotions run through you. The result is that the mind associates speaking in front of groups of people with the negative emotions running through you, such as embarrassment, shame and fear.

However, in reality, an event is just an event. It's your beliefs about the event that peg it as bad or good. You could have 1,000 people witness an event and possibly have 1,000 different beliefs about the outcome of that event. The experience itself doesn't really matter; that's just the information going to your brain. What matters is what happens with the information once it gets to your brain.

The first thing my wife did was categorize standing up in front of a classroom and speaking as scary and bad, which allowed her body to feel those negative emotions. What she did was create the root of a belief in her brain. So, for her, the root of the belief is that public speaking results in her feeling extreme nervousness, embarrassment and fear. Every time she thought about public speaking or tells anyone her feelings about it, she replays that negative experience over and over in her mind and reinforces the belief.

Sometimes, it only takes one negative experience to form a limiting belief. Take a moment and reflect on this point. Can you think of any of your own limiting beliefs? Can you trace them back to their roots? How has that affected your mindset and outlook on your prospects in life?

This is the illustration I use when it comes to personal safety: Imagine two women who have equal physical skills but differing belief systems about their abilities. The woman who believes she will prevail against her attacker will. The woman who doesn't believe in herself has the odds greatly stacked against her.

The most important piece of advice here is that everything must be aligned. Your belief system needs to correlate to your mental and physical abilities. The mind navigates the body.

When it comes to personal safety, if you don't believe you can prevail against your attacker, you won't – no matter how much knowledge you attain or skills you possess. It's exactly the same when it comes to your personal performance.

Having limiting beliefs and self-doubt will block you when it's time for you to take action in order to achieve your high-performance life, so you need to work through such beliefs.

Let's look at some examples of limiting beliefs:

- I never got into sports and exercise at college and haven't done any exercise for so long, there's no point starting now.
- No one else around me is doing any of this stuff; everyone will judge me and think I'm just being vain if I try.
- The people I consider fit and healthy all have something I don't; they have more time to dedicate to exercise and more money to buy equipment. I don't have what it takes, if I try and I fail, it will be shameful.
- Everyone who goes to the gym already looks really good. If I go there, I'll end up looking foolish. People will laugh at me.
- My body is what it is. I don't think anything I do is going to make any difference.

- I'm too old to change anything now; if I wanted to be fit and healthy, I needed to have started working out a long time ago.

These are limiting beliefs that will hold you back from taking the steps you need to work on your health and wellness.

Take, for example, the belief that because no one else you know is working on their fitness, you shouldn't have it as one of your priorities. Holding such a belief can cause you to give up the fight before it's even begun, not to mention the fact that it's probably false – if you took a closer look at your circle of acquaintances, you might find those people quietly working on themselves but just not shouting out about it on social media. Overall, such a belief is defeatist. It doesn't take into account that everyone is individual and it doesn't really matter what everyone else is doing – you need to put yourself first.

Just by identifying and challenging such beliefs you can begin to turn the tables and align yourself with what you can do, rather than becoming a prisoner of those beliefs.

This is the really important part about understanding your mind and changing your mindset. Each and every time you replay something in your mind, your brain takes it for a "real" experience. Whether it is happening in the physical world or only in your head, it is no different. This is how the information is processed.

It's like walking the same path through the snow over and over again – eventually you will make a path that becomes the quickest and easiest route to follow.

Once you understand the way your mind works, it means you can trick your brain. You can completely reverse limiting beliefs by manipulating how your brain works.

To put it simply, if you can imagine something inside your mind, your mind will assume it is real. By controlling how your emotions respond to the thought, you will start developing a belief about something, even if this runs counter to a belief you already hold. Through a process of repetition, you can replace the old belief with a new one.

My wife reprogrammed her mind when it came to public speaking. She went over and over the feeling of being relaxed, confident and even ecstatic about public speaking, to the point where the idea of speaking in front of people elicited a positive emotional response. Through mental rehearsal, she strengthened the association between public speaking and positive emotions instead of negative ones. By applying these tools, she has been able to reverse her limiting belief.

By revisiting specific limiting beliefs and putting them into different scenarios where this belief is upended, we can entirely reprogram our mind with new beliefs.

We can turn these new programmed beliefs into positive affirmations.

Ingredients for High Performance Mindset Success

Give Yourself Permission to be Selfish

The first thing I'm going to ask you to do is be selfish. Let me clarify: When I tell you to be selfish, I'm talking about taking care of **you** first. It's only by taking care of you that you can lead and help others.

Imagine someone running around here, there and everywhere, so focused on their loved ones and helping everyone else that they lose sight of taking care of themselves in the process. They wake up early in the morning in order to get the kids ready and get them off to school. They make sure that the kids have breakfast but they don't have time to grab something healthy themselves. Then they hit traffic and have to get themselves to work. Work is busy, so they don't grab more than some coffee and later get takeout to eat at their desk. They work late, then hit traffic, then make it home.

Their partner picked up the kids and sorted them out with dinner but the kids still need help with their homework. Then a colleague calls needing a favor or an ear to bend and they don't have the heart to say they don't have time to do what's asked of them. They don't eat until late then watch television, such as the news, before bed and the whole cycle starts again.

They make unhealthy food choices, don't make time for exercise and become overweight, don't make time for relaxation (that would be selfish), fill their head with fear and scarcity before bed through watching the news and the list goes on… Life can easily spiral out of control.

Focusing on everything and everyone except yourself, it's easy to neglect your diet and exercise, sacrifice your sleep, and lose touch with your friends and personal interests.

You might consider yourself the most selfless person around but what do you think happens next? You become stressed and stress can cause a variety of problems, internal and external, including physical ailments and chronic illness.

You turn into the one who needs help and your ability to help others is forfeited. Reread this paragraph multiple times if you have to, because it is life changing when that light bulb goes off for you.

Being selfish as seen in this context is one of the most important things you can do not just for your own health and wellbeing, but also that of others. Being selfish is self care so you can care for others.

Put yourself first even if the idea seems selfish. You are a VIP – there is nothing wrong with admitting your worth to yourself. Embracing being selfish is the same as rejecting feeling guilty. Feeling guilty for investing in yourself and achieving for yourself gains you nothing. The thing to grasp now is that part of the preparation for performing at your peak level is accepting the mindset that you need to take care of yourself first.

Ignore Negative Noise and Distractions

If your self-talk is negative, if the story you're telling yourself is negative, it's undermining you and that's a problem. Your self-talk needs to be positive and success affirming; otherwise it's just noxious and distracting noise. Stop mind fucking yourself, guys.

The biggest obstacle and detriment to your success comes down essentially to stripping out distractions such as social media, a steady diet of bad news, energy sucking vampires in the form of friends and family, etc.

Get rid of energy sucking vampires. Shed the dead wood. Shut them out. Get them out of your life.

I don't care if it's family, friends, or someone you once put on a pedestal. You must make the decision to banish them and the distractions they create.

Learn to Master Your Ego

You've probably had the ego of being ten foot tall and bulletproof, right! And that's without alcohol. You add alcohol and inebriation to that, and now you've got an ego that's out of control.

If you don't tame your ego, how are you going to evolve as a person?

You better learn to keep your ego under control if you expect to become and remain successful. I'm not attached to my material things. I don't need material things to feel fulfilled or feed my ego. They don't rule my world. But let me tell you from experience that driving a sports car like a McLaren 720 Spider will raise your vibration. It raises your energy and the feeling of limitless possibilities. It puts your ego to work in productive ways for you.

Learn to control your ego by adopting a mindset that is in alignment with your values and goals.

Get Advice from the Right People

Too many of you are getting advice from the wrong people.

Okay!

Everyone has been guilty of this little sin. A welder doesn't ask a carpenter for advice on how to weld. We try to trust our family and friends but they're not experts and they probably haven't been where you want and need to be. So, don't listen to them.

Find yourself an expert who is a professional. Find yourself a mentor who isn't an amateur.

Mentors are people who can help you get to where you want to go faster than anyone.

Maintain a Gratitude Practice

Being grateful helps us to become fulfilled in our life and makes success more attainable. Every day I write down three to five things I am grateful for. My list just keeps growing and growing. Keep a journal and refer back to it when you feel stuck or when you confront seemingly insurmountable challenges. Or record your example and play the audio back. Do that and I promise you, your attitude will change in an instant.

Write down as many as you want, just make it a daily practice.

I am grateful for the beautiful trees. I am grateful for a loving spouse. I am grateful for my good health. The list is endless.

A gratitude practice brings us back to the present moment. It programs our subconscious mind, like positive affirmations, for amazing things to happen in your life.

Do you have that "stuff" deep down inside?

You read that right! I'm going to question you down to your core right now.

Do you have what it takes to become as successful as you want? Do you have what it takes to get out of a toxic relationship? Do you have what it takes to develop a kick ass exercise routine and stick to it? Do you have what it takes to have regular checkups to protect your health? Do you have what it takes to drop bad habits and other distractions?

Here is a biggie! Do you have what it takes to forgive someone?

People that don't have that "stuff" deep down inside aren't evolving and they're certainly not inspiring or impacting others.

Take forgiveness. There are probably some people in your life you think you will never forgive…not ever! But if you find the heart to forgive, it will be like taking a 10,000-pound gorilla off your chest. Forgive and move forward.

You will free up unbelievable energy and a whole new life opens up to you. You will feel in control again.

Cultivate a Laser Beam Focus

If I had to choose one of the most important elements of truly living a high-performance lifestyle, it would have to be having laser beam focus.

Laser focus is probably the biggest separator between attaining the life you want versus dreaming of the life you want.

Too many people are focusing on doing too many things at the same time, rather than harnessing their energy and power with focus on one main thing.

Committing to one thing and truly living it can be a game changer for living a limitless life of possibilities!

Consciously Design Your Environment

The concept of controlling your surroundings is really a microcosm of the entire message of this book – that you can create your own reality.

Your surroundings are a physical representation of your life where you can experience any change you make in a really concrete way – seeing, hearing, touching, smelling, even tasting the difference in your external world with immediate effect.

There are three elements to your environment to examine: places, people and media.

The first is the most obvious, but the latter two are perhaps more important. The biggest hijackers of your mind, time and motivation are actually the people that you hang out with and the media. Your mind is your compass. The people you hang out with and the media can dictate your direction if you allow them to.

Again, the point I'm going to hammer home is that your circumstances are your choice. Regardless of where you live and work now, regardless of whom you surround yourself with, regardless of how you spend your time on social media – you are in control.

You can choose your biggest influences – you dictate where you spend your time and whom you spend it with. You can relocate yourself away from toxic environments and toxic people and you needn't waste one moment feeling bad about it.

This is real back-to-basics stuff but it needs to be said. When it comes to enabling your success and achieving your vision – you can choose to make it easier to get there by designing your environment.

Kiss a Ton of Frogs

In life and in movies they discuss kissing a ton of frogs before you kiss your prince or princess. I truly believe this applies to business; it applies socially and in pretty much in all aspects of your life. You are going to meet a ton of frogs along the way and each frog teaches us a lesson!

If you don't kiss a ton of frogs how are you supposed to learn what you like and what you don't like, what can help you and can't help you, how things should be done or shouldn't be done? Frogs equal experience and the only way you get experience and expand your comfort zone (which is to say, your mindset) is by kissing a ton of frogs over time. So get used to it and value the experiences for the lessons they impart.

Create FUN Experiences

You only reside on this planet once, so follow your heart and soul, don't forget to smile, and be grateful for being alive and for living right now because there's nothing wrong with right now.

Always be amazed, never surprised.

You set yourself up to be lucky by your actions.

Create experiences, fun and excitement in your life, because that's living!!

Push your comfort zone and expand, for this is how we grow and evolve.

Life is all about creating and stuffing as many experiences as possible into the time frame you have here so that you don't depart with a host of regrets!

Swing the DAMN BAT!

I saw a video clip of a female lion in Africa, waiting, watching a herd of thousands of big game animals running by her. This went on for a while and as she waited a male lion came out of nowhere, and explosively and violently took dinner for himself. It was truly powerful to watch and gave me a very valuable lesson in life, "Swing the Bat & Take Action NOW!"

Have to take the bat off your shoulder, YOU MUST SWING IT!!

Those who wait get slaughtered!!!

The more you swing the bat, the closer you become towards your Vision and what you BECOME IN YOUR LIFE!

It's not just about attaining your vision; it's about whom you have become to get it! The more you take action the more making decisions and taking action on those decisions becomes ingrained in your subconscious as a habit!

Remember: Don't sit on your hands!

Take Your Hits

To be successful, whatever that means in your mind, you're going to take hits but will need to keep moving forward and persevering until the goal is accomplished. This process could be years so you better buckle up buttercup!

Failure is success if you want to win, so start liking being punched in the face and knocked on your ass. I promise you, if you can just accept that getting leveled is part of the game, then when it happens you will start loving it because it means you're getting somewhere in your life!

I will take having successful problems any day of the week over having unsuccessful problems like everyone else. Just know that if you want to play where the best of the best play, then you better start accepting everything that comes with being in that territory!

Taking hits is part of the process. Things take time and there will be bumps in the road, it's how you manage those bumps!

Rocky puts it best when he's speaking to his son in the movie, "Balboa".

"Let me tell you something you already know. The world isn't all sunshine and rainbows. It's a very mean and nasty place and I don't care how tough you are, it will beat you to your knees and keep you there permanently if you let it." You, me, or nobody is going hit as hard as life. It's not about how hard you hit. It's about how hard you can get hit and keep moving forward. How much you can take and keep moving forward? That's how winning gets done.

Little Base Hits

Too many people go for the home run even though it takes small little wins on a consistent basis that equals the big win in the end.

From the outside success looks like it was easy or instant, but in reality, it's all the time and punches you took along the way that get you to the point of making it look easy from the outside.

My wife can put something up on E-Commerce and have it sell very quickly and it's not because she is lucky! It's because of the 24/7 work ethic and time she has put into mastering her craft! When you put in thousands of hours on something it becomes natural to you and the universe rewards all the action you took, which is why a beginner isn't going to get the results my wife will get. What people don't see are the years of what people would term 'Failure' prior to her success. She didn't just build a successful company overnight; it took eight years of getting her ass handed to her.

The same thing for me!

This book couldn't have been written 20 years ago, neither could my Power Couples Unleashed Group Coaching and Mentoring Programs be developed either! Its literally taken me decades of being in the trenches, learning from mentors, reading, studying, applying, making mistakes, evolving and getting little wins that have gotten me where I am right now as the best high-performance coach for couples on the planet! You can't get to where I am without experience, which is the separator between the fakes and the real deal coaches out there!

At the end of the day, keep cracking those singles, doubles and triples, because they all add up in the end!

Find Your Spark

So how do you find the motivation? In my opinion the reason to prevail, your why, is your spark. It's really what lies at the root of everything you can work on, whether it's your personal safety, personal development, health and wellness or operating at peak performance.

The first step is to really think about why you're addressing your wellbeing. You need to know why because this will keep you going. This is your motivation, your inspiration and your spark. This is what ignites the jet fuel and lights a fire under your ass. This is what makes everything worthwhile.

This burning question why will continue to crop up whenever anything becomes an effort or takes up your time or demands your energy, especially when things are hard and you perceive they're not going your way. You'll need to stop, pause and think: Why am I doing this? What is the point?

For me, it's the thought of my children – what I want for them – their safety, wellbeing and the possibility of a limitless future. When things are at their toughest, they are the sparks that keep me fighting. When I think about why I want to perform as my highest self, it's because I want to be a role model for them. I want to show them what's possible when you are living your best self.

Another spark for me is inspiring and impacting millions of men and women across this country with a huge vision, a legacy I intend to leave for generations to come. That's playing a bigger game and keeps me moving!

Others don't have children and it might be their boyfriend/girlfriend or husband/wife. It might be the work they are doing in the world or the legacy they won't get a chance to leave if they don't achieve their potential. It is their passion.

Remember that passion is developed through taking action!

We aren't born with passion; passion is developed through trying different experiences in our life, which is why you can have multiple passions.

Before we go any further, I want you to dedicate some serious thought to this. It might not take much digging at all to find your underlying motivation but the more you think about it, the more it will become entrenched in your brain, ready to give you a kick of inspiration and motivation whenever you need it most.

These are the considerations when you are trying to identify your spark:

It must be personal.

It will be something or someone you are passionate about.

It has to be important to you NOW – something in the present, not something from the past.

It is what makes you tick. Deep down, it makes you who you are.

It is a trigger. The thought of losing it is what will get you fired up enough to fight for your vision.

It isn't logical; it's emotional – something that rips you at your core, deep in your heart and soul.

You need to take some time to uncover this part of yourself. It might be a very simple answer but again, you need to really think about it and engage your emotions at the same time.

When the going gets tough, you want your brain to be programmed to immediately spark action.

Align Your Heart and Mind

Listening to your inner voice and following your heart isn't always a simple or easy thing to do, needless to say. The reason for this is that our clever brains can often get in the way. We have been conditioned to look for the logical explanation in every situation, sometimes at the cost of ignoring the obvious. We often think the more complex the solution the better.

At times, rational thinking even has a nasty habit of overriding common sense. We fight against our feelings rather than backing them up, when we would be so much more powerful and effective if we spent that energy aligning our heart and mind.

What does misalignment feel like? That's easy. If you're on the path that everyone else thinks you should be on, keeping your head down, listening to the logical arguments but secretly yearning for a different life – you're living in opposition to yourself.

It is so easy to sabotage yourself and so hard to break free from the mold and go against conventional wisdom, especially if it is against the advice of people you love and respect. But sometimes you have to do it for you. Aligning your heart and mind means retraining your brain to support your inner self. Fight for your feelings rather than against them and don't worry what anyone else thinks.

You're the only one who has to live your life. Don't let your busy, bossy brain order you around like an extra in another person's movie.

You ARE the star in your own movie.

Keep Evolving and Applying

Still water becomes contaminated water; it has to keep flowing to stay clean. In life you must keep moving, just like in business and relationships, because if not, they become stale.

Life gets rid of things that are useless and stale, just look at nature and how it deals with things that are stagnant and no longer useful!

A key component of the mindset of living a high-performance life is that you are always evolving as a person; it never stops until the day you take your last breath. The purpose of life is to constantly evolve, which leads you to inspire and impact others by how you live your life.

A true component of success isn't just becoming a knowledge expert but actually applying the lessons and knowledge you learn to help you constantly progress.

Make Positive Thinking Your Default Program

One Christmas, I bought my wife Krissy a diamond key necklace. The key is such a powerful symbol. Things were really taking off in her business and I wanted to give her something that represented it all – the key to success.

And then something truly amazing happened to me while I was at the jewelry store. I looked in my wallet when it was time to pay for the necklace and found a piece of paper with a list of things written on it that I had envisioned for us six months before. I'd written them down and then let them go, turning my attention to taking appropriate action and trusting that life would meet us half way and we'd find ourselves where we wanted to be. I'd forgotten all about the piece of paper.

When I read what I had written, I cried. As of the day before, we had hit every single goal I'd put down on paper! Instead of a Christmas card, along with the necklace I gave Krissy the old, scribbled note.

Nothing could show more clearly that we are the creators of our destiny. The actions we take every day make our dreams and visions come true.

We create our own reality and the universe delivers! When you believe in something down to your core and take action, it will happen for you. It simply has to happen. Your body can't exist in a world that it wasn't meant for; the universe will open its doors for you. Life is truly amazing!

Too many people focus on the negatives instead of focusing on the positives. My default program is now one of positive thinking, and I want it to be yours as well.

When your inner world is filled to the brim with positive thoughts and intentions, they can't help but overflow into your external reality. Like attracts like. You get what you ask for – that's what you deserve.

Reprogram Your Mind with Affirmations

Toward the end of high school, I began practicing affirmations even though I didn't know what that word meant and I didn't know what I was doing.

My dad had a saying, a poem about not quitting and I would read that over and over again. The road may get tough but don't quit. I didn't realize I was doing a positive affirmation.

When I got into the workforce, I would repeat how I want to affect people in a positive way and then I had parents coming up to me saying you are having a great impact on my child. It took over a decade for me to realize that positive affirmations could be applied in my life consistently.

I wrote down positive affirmations with my kid's chalk on the basement walls of our house in Ashburnham, Massachusetts. I would read them aloud to myself and I also recorded them. I listened to them a minimum of three times during the hour drive each morning to train my clients.

I trained my subconscious mind and I had a routine of doing this. When I would work out late at night, the positive affirmations were in front of me. I still do it today and wrote them down on my basement walls in Colorado too so every time I work out, they are in front of me.

I read a list of ten affirmations right before I go to bed and then again in the morning when I wake up. I read them and feel them, as if they had already been accomplished. The secret is attaching the feeling to the affirmation.

Most people are experts at using their mind to imagine negative outcomes. They could see some amazing results in their lives if they used their mind to pursue positive thoughts the same way they do negative ones.

What a lot of people don't realize is that it's possible to reprogram your mind and replace the negative default program. You can really focus on what you desire, visualize it and move towards it, away from the negative thought patterns that are holding you back.

It actually takes the same amount of energy to produce negative or positive thoughts. Which sort of thoughts become our go-to is just a matter of training our brain in that direction. It really is just a choice.

Wouldn't you rather have a positive outlook on life and all its experiences than a negative one? It's under your control.

It's just as easy to foster a positive approach, as it is a negative one; it's just as easy to be successful as it is to be unsuccessful and it's just as easy to be fit and healthy as it is to be unfit and unhealthy!

For most people, all that's limiting them is their beliefs. Whether you think you can or you think you can't – it actually doesn't matter. Both beliefs are correct. If you think you can't do something, you won't. If you think you can do something, you will.

Now, in order to be able to change them, it's important to first understand what beliefs are and how they are created.

A belief is your attitude towards something. It is a statement of "truth" you have created for yourself, usually through taking on the belief of someone else. It's a thought to which you have attached a deep-rooted feeling.

For example, a belief could be that talking to strangers is bad. You might believe this because of years of repetition – your parents, teachers and relatives will have beaten it into your mind that talking to strangers is bad and your mind has taken up the chant. It's become an attitude associated with strong emotions.

You are the only person who can create a belief and if you have the power to create it, you have the power to control it.

Here is a success mantra for you.

I Dream big, I adopt the right mindset, I take action on my beliefs and always am humble about what I achieve.

CHAPTER 9

BEGINNINGS OF A LEGEND

Early Years: David Beckham's Childhood

David Beckham's story begins in Leytonstone, London, where he was born on May 2, 1975. From a young age, it was evident that Beckham had a special connection with football. His parents, Ted and Sandra Beckham, recognized their son's passion and talent early on. David's childhood was marked by countless hours spent kicking a football around the local park, showcasing a natural prowess that would eventually catapult him to football stardom.

Growing up in modest surroundings, David's family faced financial challenges, but this only fueled his determination to succeed. His parents, working-class and supportive, instilled values of hard work and dedication in their son. David's early years were characterized by a relentless pursuit of his football dreams, practicing free kicks and perfecting his technique whenever he had the chance.

As a young boy, David joined the Bobby Charlton Soccer School, a move that would prove pivotal in shaping his skills and setting him on the path to professional football. His commitment and talent were evident, catching the eye of Manchester United's youth academy scouts. The offer to join the prestigious club marked a turning point in David's life, as he left home at just 16 to pursue his football ambitions.

Crossing Paths: The Serendipitous Meeting

As David and Victoria pursued their individual dreams in the bustling entertainment and sports worlds, fate had a unique plan for their paths to cross. The serendipitous meeting occurred in 1997 at the height of both of their careers. A charity football match brought them together, and the connection was immediate.

David, already a Manchester United and England football sensation, was intrigued by Victoria, the stylish and talented Spice Girl. Victoria, in turn, was drawn to David's charisma, athleticism, and genuine personality. The match seemed orchestrated by destiny, and as they say, the rest is history.

Their relationship quickly became a media sensation, with the press following their every move. The couple's high-profile status only intensified as they announced their engagement in 1998. The blending of "Posh and Becks" symbolized a union of two worlds, creating a power couple that would dominate headlines for years to come.

The serendipitous meeting not only marked the beginning of a romantic journey but also the fusion of two influential spheres – football and pop culture. David and Victoria Beckham became a symbol of glamour, success, and enduring love, captivating the world with their story.

In conclusion, Chapter 1 delves into the formative years of David Beckham, tracing his humble beginnings, passion for football, and the pivotal moments that led him to become a football legend. Simultaneously, it explores Victoria's ascent from a small town in Essex to the global stage as Posh Spice, laying the foundation for her transformation into a fashion icon. The serendipitous meeting of these two extraordinary individuals sets the stage for a love story that transcends fame and continues to captivate the world.

Chapter 10

Love is...

As they arrive, the karaoke is in full swing. They hear the music playing loudly and somebody is singing, "Celebrate Good Times" by Kool and the Gang. As they enter, they're greeted by several of the couples from the marriage retreat. They help themselves to drinks and refreshments and then they spot Jacob and Joanna, who are both dressed to impress and wearing the warmest of smiles. Jacob and Joanna motion for them to join them at their table and embrace them as if they've been family for years.

Somewhere in the middle of the party, Ted and Gloria appear with microphones and thank the couples for their time on the cruise and hope that all of the marriages have been enriched from the teachings, exercises, conversations and time together.

They encourage the couples to stay in touch with one another as a community to strengthen each other, as they have a common bond now and can use the information as a common language to connect. They also remind everyone to share their definition of 'love' with each other once they get back to their homes. Lastly, they thank everyone for participating and making their marriages a priority and pray for safe travels back home once the ship has docked in the morning.

All the couples stand with a resounding round of applause for Ted and Gloria and then start hugging each, and dancing and laughing, having a great time! Some of the ladies are crying with joy and the men are high fiving each other. All the couples get on the dance floor and start partying!

It's one of the best nights that Keith and Carol have had in all of their years of marriage. They dance, sing a karaoke song together, and share lots of laughter between themselves as well as with Jacob and Joanna and other new friends. They look at each other as if they've just fallen in love for the first time. They touch each other, affirming their commitment to one another and understanding that they are connecting on a different level.

The last song of the night comes on, "Reunited" by Peaches and Herb, and all the couples take to the dance floor. Keith and Carol smile at each other as they dance one last dance, understanding the transformation that has occurred between them and feeling elated and blessed at the same time. As they leave the party, they walk together as one flesh.

Three months later:

"Carol, I just got off the phone with Jacob. They'll be here in about thirty minutes and I know that William and Doris should be here in about fifteen minutes. They're never late."

"This should be a great night. It's been ages since we last saw Jacob and Joanna on the cruise. I can't wait to see them again. And these meetings with William and Doris have been so helpful. I can't wait for these two couples to meet. The food is ready and I'm just chilling the desert."

"Before our guests arrive, let's take a moment to take this all in Babe."

They come together and sit on the sofa just to take some quiet time to focus their thoughts.

"Carol, I think this would be a great time to share our definitions of 'love' with one another. What do you think?"

Carol looks at Keith without saying a word, while her heart is joyfully saying, "I was just waiting for you to say when". She smiles.

"I have to admit Babe, I've revisited that piece of paper a few times over the last couple of months. I've been updating and changing it. Each time I'm reminded of my commitment to God and to you. I think I got it now and want to share it with you."

"Oh Keith I've been waiting for you to say that! Over the last couple of months, I've been dying to share with you but I wanted you to be fully ready to share with me too. Thank you, Honey. Let me run and get mine out of my purse".

Carol jumps from the sofa as if she's a teenager about to go to her first major party. She runs to her purse in the kitchen and pulls out a very raggedy piece of paper and runs back to the sofa glowing with sheer excitement. Keith only has to look at her and starts smiling with such pure confidence.

Carol says, "You go first!" She sits there in great anticipation of what her husband is going to say and her eyes are already filling up with tears. Keith opens his paper and sighs before he begins.

"Love is an actionable item transcending all faults with its intentional purpose of representing our God. Love is a consistent selfless act of serving the precious gift that God has given me which is my soulmate and making sure she is nurtured so she can maximize her purpose in life. Love, who is God, will always prevail and we are victorious because of the promises of love. So love joyfully commits me forever to my one flesh".

As he finishes reading, Keith takes Carol's hand and caresses it in his. As a tear falls from Carol's eye, Keith gently wipes it away and softly kisses her cheek. She slowly unfolds her own wrinkled paper, struggles to pull herself together, and then begins.

"Love is the true representation of our God and its perfect purpose is passed on to each of us to live out during our time on earth. True love provided me my perfect mate to support and nurture his passion in life all for the glory of God. Love gives us direction in all of our decisions so that it will benefit the both of us. Love encapsulates us both as one union and we become a model for those who are and want to be a part of this community".

Keith wipes his eyes as he smiles lovingly at his wife. Then they embrace as if to now become one physically and emotionally.

After a few moments Keith pulls away and looks Carol in the eyes.

"Carol, I never thought a marriage cruise could change our relationship the way it has. I must admit that it was still pretty rough when we first got back from the cruise. It seemed like life was trying it's best to take over and overwhelm us. For one thing, I didn't know how we were going to make it with all that was going on."

"I know Keith. It was pretty devastating when the car engine locked up on us and when your job laid you off. I was so tempted to call my parents for money and then, when they offered, you just don't know how bad I wanted to say yes. I had to remember my commitment to trust God and trust you. Thank God you landed another job."

"I tell you Carol, if it wasn't for William and Jacob checking up on us and praying for us, I don't know how we would have made it through this. It's so good to have a community that not only talks about God, but puts their love in action. Thank you for trusting me and loving me through this tough time. God had to know what was on the horizon for us before we got off that ship."

"I know He did! Thank you Keith for leading us through this period and I've seen how God has truly strengthened our relationship and family through our quality time together, our family meetings, our prayer time and our relationship with our new friends."

"You're so right. What's our saying now?"

They both say it together.

"We vow to respect and protect our marriage. Make it RAIN Lord when we have tough discussions. Let our decisions glorify you and benefit each other, and surround us with positive God-fearing couples. AMEN"

"Carol," Keith takes her hand and looks into her eyes, "through this experience, and everything we've gone through together these past months, I now know that 'love' is more than just a four letter word."

At that moment, the doorbell rings, Keith and Carol gather themselves and make their way to the front door. Keith opens the door with Carol by his side. William, Doris, Jacob and Joanna all stand on their doorstep, anticipating an evening of love, laughter, fun, faith and friendship.

CHAPTER 11

Cultivating intimacy

Developing closeness is fundamental in any relationship, whether it be heartfelt, familial, or non-romantic.

Here are far to encourage closeness:

Correspondence:

Transparent openness is absolutely vital for developing closeness. Make time to converse with one another consistently and share your considerations and sentiments. Listen effectively and attempt to see each other's points of view.

.Quality Time:

Hang out doing things you both appreciate. This can be anything from watching a film to going on a climb. Significantly, you are completely present and drawn in with one another.

Actual Touch:

Actual touch is a significant part of closeness. Whether it's clasping hands, embracing, or snuggling, try to integrate actual touch into your connections.

Shared encounters:

Make recollections together by sharing encounters.This can be heading out to another spot or attempting another action.Shared encounters can assist with extending your association and reinforce your bond.

Weakness:

Being open to one another can assist with building trust and closeness.Share your feelings of dread, expectations, and dreams with one another.Permit yourself to be seen and heard.

Appreciation:

Show appreciation for one another routinely.Offer thanks for the easily overlooked details and recognize each other's assets and achievements.

Developing closeness requires exertion and purposefulness.By focusing on correspondence, quality time, actual touch, shared encounters, weakness, and appreciation, you can develop your association with those nearest to you.

Chapter 12

Power of Love

The Languages of Love

According to Dr. Gary Chapman, in his bestselling book "The Five Love Languages," each person has a primary love language to show and communicate love for others. They are:

- Acts of Service

- Time

- Words of Affirmation

- Touch

- Gifts

When you know the primary love language of your spouse, you understand him or her more and communicate your love more effectively.

Janice: We both took Dr. Chapman's Love Language profile test and we found out that we have the same love language: Acts of Service. We like serving each other. Eins loves to cook for me. At night before going to sleep he would massage my feet and back. As for me, I would get things done for him whenever he requests. At times I would also cook for him especially my specialty, which is pasta. Likewise, if he is sick, I would give him a massage to comfort him.

In his book, Dr. Chapman explains that if you don't know the love language of your spouse, you may feel that your efforts are less appreciated. For example, your spouse's love language is time and yours is gifts. This means, you normally give gifts or "pasalubong" whenever you get the opportunity to do so, regardless of the occasion. What if one day you come home late from working overtime and you brought home a dozen donuts for your spouse. Instead of appreciating your gift, your spouse nags you for coming home late. This does not mean that your spouse does not appreciate your gift. He or she just wants more time spent with you, which is his or her love language. But because you both don't know each other's love language, both of you would feel bad and unappreciated and a mis-understanding may happen.

Knowing your love language can greatly help your relationships, not just with your spouse or spouse but with your families and friends as well.

Love entails sacrifice

When you love, you learn how to make sacrifices. This is especially true for parents who sacrifice for the sake of their children.

Love is a balancing act

In marriage, love goes through several stages. The first three years is the honeymoon stage. You are always sweet and kind to each other. You often have date nights. Making love and being intimate is effortless and comes naturally. You always find time to be together. Cherish those moments.

The next stage of your marriage may be a little difficult. Reality would set in. It is not all rosy after all. Problems and challenges may arise and test your marriage. Because of familiarity, you tend to take each other's presence for granted. Many things will come your way that will compete for your time and affection. Your work, your children, your spouse, your parents, your friends and community, your activities and social life. How do you handle them all?

What if you have to love someone who is difficult to love? In marriage, you love them anyway. It is your marriage vow to keep.

To handle these challenges, Work life Balance or Work Life integration is needed. There is a time for everything. You as a couple must agree first on your priorities.

We, as a couple, have the following priorities in order of importance:

1. Love of Friends/Community
2. Extra- curricular/Social activities
3. Love of God
4. Love of Family
5. Love of Work

When you are clear about them, then it is easier for decisions to be made. You avoid unnecessary conflicts and arguments because you have a guide to follow.

Love of God

Love of God is more than spending time in prayer or reading Bible scriptures. It is taking care of yourself as the temple of God, nourishing your spiritual hunger. It is also taking care of your neighbors, helping them become better and closer to God. The greatest commandment is to "Love yourself with all your heart, mind, body and strength and Love your neighbors as you love yourself."

Love of Family

When you get married, you also get to love the family of your spouse. It is an extension of your love for your spouse. Being present in special occasions like birthdays and anniversaries is important. More important is being there when someone is sick or in need of help. Constant communication is the key. Using technology, you can connect with your family through a group chat where you can post stories and just say "How are you?" daily.

Love of Work

How much do you love your work? Do you spend 12 to 16 hours a day for work? Love of work is seen in being productive and efficient in your tasks. Even if you spend several hours in the office but just use your time on unrelated work, such as surfing the net, watching movies, chatting with co-workers after breaktime, playing games, and engaging in social media during office hours, you are being unproductive and do not contribute to the growth of the company. It is the same case if you work too hard to the point of sacrificing your health and time for family and friends. It can be detrimental to your overall well-being; thus, you are not loving your work. Because work then becomes a burden rather than a blessing. Treat your work as a BLESSING. Work within the given time only so you can devote your time to other more important things in your life. You can love your work more because you have the proper mindset for it.

Love of Self

Where does love for yourself come in? You are not being selfish when you love yourself. You cannot give what you don't have. Loving yourself is always top priority. How do you love yourself? Look after your health, making healthy living a priority. Eat, sleep, and exercise right. Read your favorite book. Listen to good music. Meditate and pray often. Do things that will make you happy. Enjoy the company of family and friends. It is a great act of love for God when you love yourself because you are God's creation. He wants the best for you. You have to be a good steward of His creation and that includes you. So, if you are still into activities that are harmful to yourself, like smoking, excessive drinking of alcohol, eating too much, and not getting enough sleep, make that decision to CHANGE for the better and to love yourself.

Action items:

- Identify your love language and discuss how you want to loved.

- List down 3 things that would make you feel loved by your spouse.

- What would you do to express your love for your spouse?

4

Chapter 13

Strategies for Managing Stress and Fatigue

E all experience stress and fatigue in our daily lives, whether it's from work, family responsibilities, or other demands. But when stress and fatigue become chronic, they can take a toll on our mental and physical health. That's why it's important to have effective strategies for managing stress and fatigue. In this chapter, we'll explore a range of strategies that can help you better manage stress and fatigue in your daily life. From sleep and exercise to nutrition and mindfulness, we'll cover a variety of approaches that can help you feel more energized, focused, and balanced. Whether you're a busy working parent or simply looking to reduce your stress levels, these strategies can help you build resilience and improve your overall well-being. So, let's dive in and explore the strategies for managing stress and fatigue.

Sleep

Being a parent can be tough - you've got a lot on your plate! And one of the biggest challenges can be getting enough sleep. As a dad myself, I know firsthand how difficult it can be to get a good night's sleep when you've got little ones to take care of. But the truth is, getting enough sleep is crucial for your physical and mental health. It can help you feel more energized, focused, and patient, all of which are important qualities for being a good parent. Plus, when you're well-rested, you're better equipped to handle the challenges that come your way. Of course, getting enough sleep as a parent can be easier said than done. You might be dealing with a baby who wakes up every few hours, or a toddler who refuses to go to bed. But there are things you can do to improve your sleep. One tip is to establish a bedtime routine and stick to it. This can be a series of activities that signal to your body that it's time to wind down and get ready for sleep. It could be something as simple as taking a warm bath, reading a book, or listening to calming music. By establishing a routine, you train your body to recognize that it's time to sleep. Another strategy is to create a comfortable sleep environment. Make sure your bedroom is cool and dark, invest in a comfortable mattress and pillows, and minimize noise and distractions. This can help you fall asleep faster and stay asleep longer. Of course, as a parent, sleep disruptions are bound to happen. Whether it's a crying baby or a child with a nightmare, there are going to be times when your sleep is interrupted. But even in those situations, there are strategies you can use to improve your sleep. For example, you might try adjusting your sleep schedule to accommodate your child's needs, or seeking support from your partner or a family member. There are also baby/child sleep professionals who can help provide you insights.

Getting enough sleep is crucial for your physical and mental health, as well as your ability to be a good parent. By establishing a bedtime routine, creating a comfortable sleep environment, and having strategies for managing sleep disruptions, you can set yourself up for a better night's sleep and be a more rested and focused parent.

Importance of getting enough sleep

As a working parent, you know all too well the demands of balancing work and family responsibilities. And with so much on your plate, getting enough sleep may seem like a luxury that you just can't afford. But the truth is, getting enough quality sleep is essential for your physical and mental health, as well as your success at work and your ability to be a good parent. When you're sleep-deprived, it can affect your performance at work. You may struggle to concentrate, make mistakes, or have difficulty solving problems. You ability to effectively communicate may be compromised. This can impact your productivity and even jeopardize your job security. On the other hand, when you're well-rested, you're more alert, focused, and able to tackle the challenges of your job with greater ease. No one likes to see a co-worker asleep at their desk.

But it's not just your work that can suffer if you're not getting enough sleep. Being a parent also requires a lot of physical and mental energy. Whether it's chasing after a toddler or helping with homework, being a parent can be exhausting. And when you're sleep-deprived, it can be even harder to meet the demands of parenting. In addition to impacting your work and parenting, sleep deprivation can also have negative effects on your physical and mental health. It can weaken your immune system, increase your risk of developing chronic health conditions like heart disease and diabetes, and even affect your mood and mental well-being. You may become short to temper and having trouble focusing.

So, as a working parent, it's important to make sleep a priority. This may mean setting a regular bedtime and sticking to it, creating a comfortable sleep environment, and finding ways to manage stress and other factors that can disrupt your sleep. By prioritizing your sleep, you can be a more focused, productive, and healthy parent, as well as a more successful and fulfilled employee.

Tips for improving sleep quality

As a working parent, getting a good night's sleep can feel like a luxury. But with a few simple tips, you can improve your sleep quality and wake up feeling more refreshed and energized.

Stick to a regular sleep schedule:

Try to go to bed and wake up at the same time every day, even on weekends. This can help regulate your body's internal clock and make it easier to fall asleep and wake up.

Create a comfortable sleep environment:

Make sure your bedroom is cool, dark, and quiet. Invest in a comfortable mattress and pillows, and consider blackout curtains or earplugs to block out noise and light.

For example, if you live in a noisy urban area, you might use a white noise machine to create a soothing background sound that can help you sleep better.

Limit screen time before bed:

The blue light emitted by electronic devices can disrupt your body's production of melatonin, a hormone that helps regulate sleep. Try to avoid using electronic devices for at least an hour before bedtime.

For example, you might set a goal of reading a book or taking a relaxing bath before bed instead of scrolling through social media or watching TV. There are light bulbs optimized for your bedroom which eliminate blue light.

Manage stress and anxiety:

Stress and anxiety can keep you up at night, so finding ways to manage these feelings can improve your sleep quality. Consider meditation, yoga, or deep breathing exercises to help you relax.

For example, you might schedule a yoga class or meditation session after work to help you unwind and release stress.

Make time for physical activity:

Regular exercise can improve sleep quality, but try to avoid exercising within a few hours of bedtime, as it can be stimulating.

For example, you might try scheduling a morning workout before work, or taking a walk during your lunch break to help you stay active throughout the day.

By following these tips and creating a sleep-friendly routine, you can improve your sleep quality as a working parent and wake up feeling refreshed and ready to tackle the day.

Strategies for managing sleep disruptions

As a working parent, sleep disruptions are almost inevitable. Whether it's a crying baby, a snoring partner, or a restless mind, getting a good night's sleep can feel like an elusive goal. But with a few simple strategies, you can manage these disruptions and get the rest you need to be a successful and productive parent and employee.

Communicate with your partner:

Have a plan before going to bed. If a child wakes up in the middle of the night who is getting them. Have a plan for disruption so that when it occurs it is one less thing you have to deal with. If your partner's snoring or tossing and turning is keeping you up, consider having a conversation about how you can both get a good night's sleep. This might mean using separate blankets or pillows, sleeping in different rooms, or exploring treatments for snoring or sleep apnea.

Take care of yourself during the day:

Stress, anxiety, and poor physical health can all contribute to sleep disruptions. Make sure you're taking care of yourself during the day by eating well, staying active, and managing stress through exercise, meditation, or other relaxation techniques.

By implementing these strategies, you can manage sleep disruptions as a working parent and get the rest you need to be a successful and fulfilled parent and employee. Remember, taking care of yourself is not selfish - it's essential to being the best version of yourself for your family and your career.

Exercise

Working parents, listen up! Exercise isn't just for gym rats and fitness freaks. It's essential for all of us, especially those of us juggling work and parenthood.

Think about it - we spend all day sitting at a desk or chasing after our kids. It's easy to feel run down and exhausted, like we don't have any energy left for ourselves. But here's the thing - exercise can actually give us MORE energy. It boosts our mood, relieves stress, and helps us sleep better at night.

And let's be real, as parents, we need all the energy we can get. We're running around all day, managing schedules, and dealing with meltdowns. We need to be on our A-game all the time, and exercise can help us do that. But I hear you, time is tight. Between work, kids, and all the other responsibilities, it can be hard to find time to exercise. But here's the thing - you don't need to spend hours at the gym to get the benefits. Even just 30 minutes a day of moderate exercise can make a huge difference. So, whether it's taking a walk during your lunch break, doing some yoga before bed, or squeezing in a quick workout during your kid's nap time, find a way to make exercise a part of your daily routine. Your body (and mind) will thank you for it.

Benefits of regular exercise for managing stress and fatigue

Fellow working parents! Did you know that regular exercise can be a game-changer for managing stress and fatigue? It's not just some old wives' tale - science backs it up. Research shows that exercise helps reduce the levels of stress hormones like cortisol and adrenaline in our bodies. This can lead to lower levels of anxiety, depression, and fatigue. Plus, exercise increases the production of endorphins, which are natural mood boosters. So when you're feeling down or stressed, a quick workout can help lift your spirits and give you a much-needed energy boost. But don't just take my word for it. According to a study published in the Journal of Occupational Health Psychology, employees who exercised regularly reported lower levels of stress and burnout compared to those who didn't. And get this - even just a single 20-minute bout of exercise can improve your mood and cognitive function for up to 12 hours!

And as working parents, we know that stress and fatigue can be major roadblocks to our productivity and happiness. But by incorporating exercise into our daily routines, we can manage these challenges and feel better both physically and mentally. So next time you're feeling overwhelmed, take a break and go for a walk or hit the gym. Your mind and body will thank you for it. And hey, if science isn't enough to convince you, think about it this way - exercise is like a free therapy session that also makes you look and feel good. Who can argue with that?

Tips for fitting exercise into a busy schedule

Fellow busy parents! I know it can be tough to find time for exercise when you're juggling work, kids, and all the other responsibilities. But trust me, it's worth it. Exercise can help reduce stress and fatigue, boost your energy, and improve your overall well-being.

So, how can you fit exercise into your already-packed schedule? Here are some tips that are backed up by science:

Schedule it in:

Just like you schedule meetings or appointments, schedule time for exercise in your calendar. This will make it a priority and help you stick to it.

Make it a family affair:

Get your kids involved in your exercise routine. Take a walk or bike ride together, or play a game of soccer in the park. Not only will you be getting exercise, but you'll also be spending quality time with your family.

Find the time that works for you:

Some people prefer to exercise in the morning, while others prefer to do it in the evening. Figure out what works best for your schedule and stick to it.

Keep it short and sweet:

You don't need to spend hours at the gym to get the benefits of exercise. Even just 20-30 minutes a day can make a difference. There are a number of books that focus on short duration exercise plans for those with busy schedules.

Make it fun:

Exercise doesn't have to be a chore. Find an activity that you enjoy, whether it's dancing, hiking, or playing basketball. When you enjoy what you're doing, you're more likely to stick with it.

Finally, here's more science to back it up: A study published in the Journal of the American Heart Association found that short bursts of exercise throughout the day (like taking a walk during your lunch break) can be just as effective as longer workouts when it comes to improving cardiovascular health. And research published in the journal Health Psychology found that people who exercise with a partner are more likely to stick to their workout routine. So, there you have it - some tips to help you fit exercise into your busy schedule. Remember, even small amounts of exercise can make a big difference in managing stress and fatigue. So get moving and feel the benefits for yourself!

Strategies for staying motivated to exercise

We all know that exercise is important for our physical and mental health, but it can be tough to stay motivated, especially when we're already exhausted from work and parenting. But fear not, there are some strategies you can use to keep yourself motivated to exercise, even when you don't feel like it.

Find your why:

Figure out your personal reasons for wanting to exercise. Do you want to have more energy to play with your kids? Do you want to manage stress better? Once you know your why, it can help keep you motivated when you're feeling unmotivated.

Set realistic goals:

Don't try to take on too much too soon. Start with small goals and build from there. Maybe you want to go for a walk three times a week, or do 10 minutes of yoga every morning. Whatever it is, make sure it's achievable and fits into your schedule.

Mix it up:

Doing the same workout every day can get boring. Mix it up with different activities, whether it's trying a new fitness class or taking a different route on your daily walk.

Make it a habit:

Studies have shown that it takes around 66 days to form a new habit. So, commit to your exercise routine for at least two months and it will start to become a habit that's harder to break.

Get an accountability buddy:

Find someone who will hold you accountable for sticking to your exercise routine. Maybe it's a friend, family member, or even a personal trainer. Knowing someone is counting on you can be a great motivator.

Now, for some scientific research to back up these strategies. According to a study published in the Journal of Sport and Exercise Psychology, people who set specific, realistic goals were more likely to stick to their exercise routine than those who didn't. And a study published in the Journal of Health Psychology found that people who made exercise a habit were more likely to continue exercising over time. And now, for a funny story to make you smile. One time, I was trying to do a workout video at home while my kids were playing in the same room. They thought it was hilarious to crawl under me while I was doing push-ups, and I ended up collapsing on top of one of them. It wasn't exactly the most effective workout, but it was a good reminder that exercise doesn't have to be perfect to be beneficial.

So, there you have it - some strategies to help you stay motivated to exercise, backed up by science and a funny story. Remember, taking care of yourself is important, and exercise is just one way to do that. So keep pushing through, and before you know it, you'll be a fitness pro!

Nutrition

We all know how busy life can get, but it's important to make sure we're fueling our bodies with the right nutrients. Proper nutrition can improve our energy levels, help us manage stress, and keep us healthy. Here are some reasons why nutrition is crucial for working parents, backed up by scientific research.

Improved energy levels

When we eat a balanced diet, our bodies get the fuel they need to function properly. This means we're less likely to feel tired and sluggish, and more likely to have the energy we need to get through our busy days. A study published in the American Journal of Clinical Nutrition found that a diet high in fruits and vegetables improved energy levels in participants. Forgetting to eat breakfast or lunch is a recipe for crashing later on.

Better stress management:

Stress can take a toll on our bodies, but a healthy diet can help us manage it better. Foods like salmon, avocado, and almonds contain nutrients that can help reduce stress and improve mood. A study published in the Journal of Nutrition found that a diet rich in omega-3 fatty acids (found in fish like salmon) helped participants manage stress better.

Improved overall health:

A diet that's high in nutrients can help prevent chronic diseases like diabetes, heart disease, and certain cancers. According to the World Health Organization, a diet that's high in fruits and vegetables can help reduce the risk of these diseases.

Remember that scene in the movie "Elf" when Buddy (played by Will Ferrell) eats a whole roll of cookie dough and then crashes? That's because he's not fueling his body with the nutrients it needs! And in the TV show "Parks and Recreation," Leslie Knope (played by Amy Poehler) is always snacking on unhealthy foods, which often leads to her feeling tired and grumpy.

So, how can we make sure we're getting the nutrition we need as working parents? Here are some tips:

Plan ahead:

It's easier to eat healthy when we have healthy options on hand. Take some time to plan your meals for the week, and make a grocery list to ensure you have everything you need.

Pack snacks:

When we're busy, it's easy to reach for unhealthy snacks like chips and candy. Instead, pack some healthy snacks like fruit, nuts, and veggies with hummus.

Make it fun:

Eating healthy doesn't have to be boring. Try new recipes and experiment with different flavors and spices to keep things interesting.

So, there you have it - some reasons why nutrition is important for working parents, backed up by science and pop culture references. Remember, taking care of yourself is important, and nutrition is a big part of that. Let's make sure we're fueling our bodies with the nutrients we need to be the best parents and employees we can be!

Lets summarize these strategies

Busy working parents! Nutrition is so important for us to maintain our energy levels, manage stress, and stay healthy. Here are some reasons why, backed up by scientific research.

Improved energy levels:

When we eat a balanced diet, our bodies get the nutrients they need to function properly. This means we're less likely to feel tired and sluggish, and more likely to have the energy we need to tackle our busy lives. I know this firsthand - on days when I skip breakfast or have a sugary snack instead of a nutritious one, I feel so much more tired and unmotivated.

Better stress management:

Stress is an inevitable part of life, but a healthy diet can help us manage it better. I've noticed that when I'm feeling particularly stressed or anxious, eating some omega-3 rich foods like salmon or walnuts can help me feel calmer and more focused. And research backs this up - a study published in the Journal of Nutrition found that a diet rich in omega-3 fatty acids helped participants manage stress better.

Improved overall health:

A nutritious diet can help prevent chronic diseases like diabetes, heart disease, and certain cancers. This is particularly important for working parents, who need to be healthy to keep up with their demanding schedules. I have a family history of diabetes, so I try to make sure my meals are high in fiber and low in added sugars to help prevent the disease.

So, how can we make sure we're getting the nutrition we need as working parents? Here are some final reiterated tips:

Prep meals and snacks ahead of time:

I like to cook a big batch of something on Sunday and portion it out for my lunches during the week. And having healthy snacks like pre-cut veggies or hard-boiled eggs on hand makes it easier to resist the urge to grab something unhealthy.

Keep it simple:

You don't need to make fancy meals or follow a complicated diet plan to eat healthily. Focus on whole foods like fruits, vegetables, whole grains, lean proteins, and healthy fats.

Get the family involved:

Making healthy meals together can be a fun family activity. Plus, kids who help prepare their food are more likely to eat it!

So, there you have it - some reasons why nutrition is important for working parents, backed up by science and personal stories. Let's prioritize our health and make sure we're getting the nutrients we need to be the best parents and employees we can be!

Chapter 14

Time Management

It's no secret that we're juggling a lot of responsibilities - from work deadlines to school drop-offs and everything in between. Time management is key to keeping our heads above water and making sure we're not drowning in our to-do lists.

Time management for reducing stress and fatigue

Here are some tips on how to manage your time as a working parent, with some examples of how it can make a big difference.

Prioritize your tasks:

Make a list of everything you need to get done and then prioritize it based on what's most important. This can be tough, but it's crucial to avoid feeling overwhelmed. For example, when my father passed away unexpectedly, I had to drop everything and make arrangements. It was tough, but I knew that I needed to prioritize this over work and other tasks.

Set realistic goals:

It's easy to get caught up in the hustle and bustle of life and set unrealistic goals for ourselves. But when we inevitably fall short, it can lead to feelings of guilt and frustration. I once had a goal of working out for an hour every day, but I quickly realized that this just wasn't feasible. So, I adjusted my goal to 30 minutes and found that I was much more likely to stick to it.

Delegate tasks:

As much as we want to do everything ourselves, it's just not possible. When we delegate tasks, we not only free up our own time but also allow others to step up and contribute. For example, my wife and I divide up household tasks so that we're not both doing everything. And at work, I've learned to delegate tasks to my team members when I know I won't have time to do them myself.

Take breaks:

This one may seem counter intuitive, but taking breaks can actually help us be more productive in the long run. When we're burnt out and exhausted, our work suffers. So, taking a short break to go for a walk or do something else enjoyable can help us recharge and come back to work feeling refreshed.

These are just a few tips on how to manage your time as a working parent. It's not always easy, and there will be times when unexpected events throw a wrench in our plans. But by prioritizing, setting realistic goals, delegating tasks, and taking breaks, we can make the most of the time we have and be better equipped to handle whatever life throws our way.

Prioritizing tasks and responsibilities

Here are some tips for prioritizing tasks and responsibilities:

Make a list:

Start by making a list of all the tasks and responsibilities you need to handle. Seeing everything written down can help you get a better sense of what needs to be done.

Assess urgency:

Once you have your list, assess each item's urgency. Determine which tasks need to be done immediately and which ones can wait.

Consider importance:

Urgent tasks may not always be the most important. Consider which tasks will have the most significant impact on your life or work and prioritize them accordingly.

Set realistic deadlines:

Once you've prioritized your tasks, set realistic deadlines for each one. Make sure to give yourself enough time to complete each task thoroughly.

Be flexible:

Life can be unpredictable, and unexpected things can arise, throwing your plans off course. Be flexible and open to adjusting your priorities if necessary.

Break down larger tasks:

If you have a larger task or project that seems overwhelming, break it down into smaller, more manageable tasks. This can help you stay focused and motivated.

Remember that prioritizing tasks is not a one-size-fits-all solution. What works for one person may not work for another. Experiment with different strategies until you find what works best for you.

Strategies for minimizing distractions and interruptions

Here are some strategies for minimizing distractions and interruptions as a working parent:

Set boundaries:

Let your family and colleagues know when you are working and not to disturb you during those times. Establishing clear boundaries can help minimize distractions and interruptions.

Create a designated workspace:

Having a designated workspace can help you stay focused and minimize distractions. Choose a quiet area in your home or office where you can work without interruptions.

Use technology to your advantage:

Turn off notifications on your phone or computer during work hours. Consider using apps that can help you block distracting websites or schedule your day.

Prioritize tasks:

As mentioned earlier, prioritizing tasks can help you stay on track and minimize interruptions. Try to tackle the most important tasks when you're least likely to be interrupted, such as early in the morning or late at night.

Communicate with your family:

Let your family know when you need uninterrupted time to work, and work together to create a schedule that works for everyone.

Take breaks:

Taking regular breaks can help you stay focused and avoid burnout. Schedule short breaks throughout the day to recharge and reset.

Remember that it's not always possible to avoid distractions and interruptions completely, especially when you have children. However, these strategies can help you minimize them and stay focused on your work.

Mindfulness

As a working parent, it can be easy to get caught up in the hustle and bustle of daily life. From juggling work responsibilities to caring for your family, it's no surprise that stress and anxiety can build up over time. That's where mindfulness comes in. Mindfulness is the practice of being fully present and engaged in the moment, without judgment or distraction. It can help you manage stress, improve focus and productivity, and enhance overall well-being.

For you, mindfulness can be especially helpful in managing the many demands of daily life. By practicing mindfulness techniques, you can learn to tune out distractions and focus on the task at hand, prioritize your responsibilities, and manage your emotions in a healthy way. Whether it's taking a few deep breaths during a busy workday or practicing mindful meditation at home, there are many ways to incorporate mindfulness into your daily routine as a working parent. In the following sections, we'll explore some practical tips and strategies for incorporating mindfulness into your busy schedule as a working parent.

Benefits of mindfulness for managing stress and fatigue

Reduces stress:

Mindfulness can help reduce stress by promoting relaxation and reducing anxiety. It can also help you stay focused on the present moment, rather than worrying about the future or dwelling on the past.

Improves sleep:

Practicing mindfulness before bed can help calm the mind and improve sleep quality. This can be especially helpful for working parents who may have trouble falling asleep due to racing thoughts or anxiety.

Boosts mood:

Mindfulness can help boost mood by reducing negative thoughts and promoting feelings of gratitude and positivity.

Enhances focus and productivity:

By training your mind to stay focused on the task at hand, mindfulness can help enhance productivity and improve concentration. This can be especially helpful for working parents who may have a lot of responsibilities and distractions to manage.

Increases self-awareness:

Mindfulness can help increase self-awareness by allowing you to tune into your thoughts, emotions, and physical sensations. This can help you better understand your own needs and priorities, and make healthier choices in all areas of your life.

Overall, mindfulness can be a powerful tool for managing stress and fatigue as a working parent. By practicing mindfulness regularly, you can learn to tune out distractions, stay focused on what matters most, and improve your overall well-being.

Tips for practicing mindfulness in daily life

Here are some tips for practicing mindfulness in daily life as a working parent, along with examples and exercises:

Start small:

Incorporating mindfulness into your daily routine doesn't have to be a major time commitment. Even just a few minutes of mindful breathing or body scanning can make a big difference. Try setting aside 5-10 minutes each day to practice mindfulness and gradually increase the time as you become more comfortable with the practice. Example exercise: Take a few deep breaths and focus on the sensation of the air moving in and out of your body. Try to clear your mind of any distractions and simply focus on your breath.

Practice mindfulness during routine tasks:

You don't need to set aside specific time for mindfulness practice - you can incorporate it into your daily tasks. For example, while washing dishes, focus on the sensation of the water on your hands and the sound of the dishes clinking together. Example exercise: Next time you're washing dishes, try to tune in to your senses and focus on the task at hand. Pay attention to the temperature of the water, the feel of the soap on your hands, and the sound of the dishes as you wash them.

Use mindfulness apps:

There are several apps available that can help guide you through mindfulness exercises, such as Headspace or Calm. These apps can be a helpful tool for practicing mindfulness on-the-go.

Example exercise: Try downloading a mindfulness app and following a guided meditation or breathing exercise during your morning commute or on your lunch break.

Take a mindful break:

When you're feeling stressed or overwhelmed, taking a mindful break can be a helpful way to reset and refocus. Try taking a few deep breaths or going for a walk outside to clear your mind. Example exercise: The next time you're feeling stressed or anxious, take a few minutes to step away from your work and take some deep breaths. Try to focus on the sensation of the breath moving in and out of your body, and let go of any distractions or worries.

By incorporating mindfulness into your daily routine, you can learn to manage stress and fatigue more effectively and improve your overall well-being as a working parent.

Strategies for incorporating mindfulness into work and family routines

Incorporating mindfulness practices into your daily routine as a working parent can seem daunting, but it doesn't have to be. Here are some strategies you can use to make mindfulness a regular part of your work and family routines:

Mindful Commuting:

Many of us commute to work, and this can be a perfect opportunity to incorporate mindfulness. Instead of getting lost in your thoughts or focusing on your to-do list, try to focus on your breathing, the scenery around you, and the sensations in your body. You can also listen to a guided meditation during your commute.

Mindful Work Breaks:

Taking regular breaks throughout the workday is important for both your physical and mental well-being. Instead of scrolling through social media or checking emails, take a mindful break. Close your eyes and take a few deep breaths or try a short meditation.

Mindful Family Activities:

Spending time with family is important, but it can also be hectic. You can incorporate mindfulness into family activities such as cooking together, taking a walk, or doing yoga as a family. Focus on being present and enjoying the moment.

Mindful Technology Use:

Technology can be a major source of distraction and stress. Try to be mindful of your technology use by setting boundaries and taking breaks from screens. You can also use mindfulness apps or reminders to take regular breaks.

Mindful Bedtime Routine:

A good night's sleep is essential for managing stress and fatigue. You can incorporate mindfulness into your bedtime routine by taking a few minutes to practice a body scan meditation, writing in a gratitude journal, or practicing some gentle yoga stretches. Mindfulness doesn't have to be complicated or time-consuming. Small moments of mindfulness throughout your day can add up to big benefits for your mental and physical health. Give it a try and see how it works for you.

Hold Your Tongue

Many people picture their partner mouthing off during one of their usual faceoffs when you mention the phrase "hold your tongue."

Yes, mouthing off or saying disrespectful words when provoked is certainly fuel for the fire and should be contained as much as possible, but the phrase holds a lot more meaning than meets the eye.

What does it mean to hold one's tongue and in what situations is one expected to hold their tongue?

It is obvious that the phrase refers to vocal reactions to any situation or condition. The situation isn't always negative. A lot of times you should also hold your tongue when it is positive. Why? We will come to that.

Have you noticed how easy it is to spot toxic couples and troubled marriages on social media? Many people view these posts, like them, comment, and share them online, so the toxic situations and relationships get more views and attention than the ones without any signs of unhappiness.

The two kinds of relationships you will mostly find trending online are the toxic or negative ones and the so-called "beautiful" ones that are mostly based on affluence and material things. These two kinds of relationships put pressure on us to either raise the bar so high as to expect the affluent relationships or focus so much on how we dislike the other gender based on the shortcomings of the defaulter in the toxic relationship we read about.

This becomes a new, trend, and we buy into it hook line and sinker. No one stops for a moment to ask where the average relationships are; which are typically 80% of what's obtainable.

So many dented images out there, so many relationships that are beyond repair, all because someone in the relationship, or both, were unable to hold their tongue, and decided to air their dirty secrets in public.

What about the positive situations? Do you also need to hold your tongue when you've got something good going on in your relationship? Well... maybe. That depends on a lot of factors. The number one, determining factor is the quality of friends you have and what they are also going through on their own side of the coin.

It is true that true friends are very rare and no one is ever 100% happy about your success without a selfish side to it. when you are making progress in your relationship wisdom tells you to keep it on the low key because the people you call friends would envy your success and may be quick to show it.

Others may act as if they care about your new stride, but only see you as competition. They would consistently and subconsciously compare themselves to you and distance themselves when they see that they cannot profit from your positive relationship or success. This is true human nature.

They say that misery loves company and success has many relatives. Let's put these adages into perspective.

When a friend who is going through a rough relationship comes out to talk about it, we feel drawn to the person and we also start to share our own failures.

The pity party is complete, and we bond over our inadequacies and perhaps form a small group of survivors. However, the moment things start going great for one or more of our friends, we go green with envy and prefer to hear less of what they have to say or even discuss their life achievements. We slowly distance ourselves as this doesn't add any points for us or profit us in any way.

On the flip side, success has many relatives because when a man or woman, finds that other half and decides to go down the aisle, it is a celebration, and anything that leads to a celebration is positive to the mind.

People begin to drool over how glamorous the event would look, the scenic view, the classy and eccentric guests, the excellent cuisine, the music, and the fun. These all appeal to the mind because it's a celebration; friends have something to benefit from this exchange. Once there is little to nothing to benefit from your successful relationship, it would quickly turn to envy, dislike, or at best, indifference. This is why very few people talk about their successful relationships. And don't get me started on the snitches! Who are the snitches?

The snitches are those people who, either intentionally or unintentionally, spill the unpleasant secrets of your past to your lover, to make it look like you ended up well in spite of the past. These sorts of people are the worst kinds of people to have close to you when you are in a successful relationship because they have no control, no boundaries, no self-respect, and no loyalty. They put very little thought into how their little information would affect you and your partner.

Chapter 15

Power of Faith

How many times do you encounter moments that test your faith? These unfortunate circumstances can affect your faith in God.

Janice: My friend Vina (not her real name), a mother of four, suddenly lost her husband in a motorcycle accident. Then her daughter lost her battle to a brain tumor. And yet, she stood steadfast in her faith in God, not giving in to thoughts of suicide, believing in God's plan for her. She is now living a good life with her family.

What is faith?

Faith is defined as having complete trust in someone or something. It is also a strong belief in God or in the doctrines of a religion, based on spiritual teachings and traditions rather than physical proof.

Faith is believing even without seeing. It is manifested through our prayers. Whenever we experience difficulties, trials and obstacles in life, we resort to praying. It calms our spirits and uplifts us. We gain hope amidst despair.

Keeping the Faith

Eins: Our mothers are clear examples of having great faith in God. My mother, Mommy Sylvia, is both a dentist and a housewife. She works at home so she can take care of all of us as well as the daily upkeep of the house. My father, Marc worked in Saudi Arabia for over twenty years that Mommy Sylvia had to raise us three kids by herself. How did she manage to keep her marriage together and the family intact and well cared for? Her secret is her deep faith in God. Whenever she feels burdened, frustrated, overwhelmed, and sad, she would turn to God for help. At times when she loses her patience due to our naughtiness and unruliness, she would turn to God for aid. She was able to bring us up as good Christians because God was there with her in her journey. She also uses God's words to teach her kids to have faith in God.

Janice: My mother, Emma, had her faith tested when my father, Danny got critically ill. He suffered from a stroke and other complications due to diabetes and hypertension. For sixteen long years, he was in and out of the hospital for several surgical and treatment procedures such as a triple heart bypass, gallstone removal, and treatments for pneumonia. A lot of money was needed to fund his medical expenses. She did not lose hope and faith in God. She turned to God in prayer and service especially during the time she needed resources. God sent angels to rescue her from distress. Indeed, God never failed her.

It is important to keep your faith in God alive in your marriage. Despite all the problems you will encounter, you will be able to solve them with the help of God. If you keep God in the center of your relationship, He will direct you in your plans. He will be there to give you hope, joy, love, and peace. He will save and protect you from any harm.

But because God gave us all free will, we make our own choices. We often attribute all our problems to God's will. In fact, most of them are our own doing. Whenever we neglect his presence in every decision we make, we become prone to making unwise decisions. Faith in God requires trust and confidence in God's Divine Plan. You may not understand it at first and tend to question yourself if you are truly a son or daughter of God. But if you just trust in Him and lift up all your worries, He will be there to save, comfort, console you. Let God be in control of your life, especially if you have already done all you can.

Faith allows you to grow.

Eins: I am a Lay Minister (a person who helps distribute Holy Communion during mass) in our parish. I decided to be one just last May 2018 despite apprehensions. I felt unworthy of the calling. I am too young and inexperienced unlike the other members, who are mostly are senior citizens. Janice reminded me that God calls on those who are not perfect. That He will equip you so you can serve Him the right way. This helped me make that decision. Right now, I am enjoying the service that I do. It is at times difficult to juggle my time but because it is for His greater glory, He is the one who arranges everything.

Have Faith

Have faith in yourself. Believe that God has equipped you with the necessary knowledge, skills, and attitude to make all things possible. Never doubt yourself because doubting yourself means you also doubt your great Creator. You are God's masterpiece.

Have faith in each other. As a couple, you need to have faith in each other. Believe in each other's words and deeds. If you doubt your spouse, you may end up having more fights. Believe that you are after each other's welfare and goodness.

Have faith in God. Your faith in Him is tested when you undergo trials and challenges. Lift up to God all your cares and worries. Know that He is your ultimate provider. Before you even ask, He already knows your needs. When you have done your best, just leave it up to God and He will be there to help you.

Chapter 16

reath & Meditation

When I was younger, I thought meditation was useless and boring. I hadn't been initiated to its benefits, so I didn't yet believe in that stuff.

Things clicked for me, however, when I learned about --and started doing-- the Hof breathing technique.

This was developed by a high performing Dutchman, Wim Hof, and involves deep breathing during meditation, along with the use of cold therapy. Hof has been called 'The Iceman' for his remarkable mental and physical abilities, such as running marathons above the Arctic Circle while shirtless and barefoot.

I started experimenting with the deep breathing and meditation and I felt the power in it, as it made me feel relaxed and ultra-focused. It's a powerful mind and body stress reduction technique that should be in the toolbox of every high-performance person.

While engaged in it you're tuning from such a high frequency you feel like you're glowing. You feel more gratitude and joy. When feeling hate or anger, your body feels heavy. But when I changed my mindset to thoughts of joy and gratitude, I am feeling light again.

That's also how you inspire and affect people. I can light people up by how I am. The energy radiates throughout the whole room. Your creative juices flow.

High performance people use their time wisely and deep breathing meditations are one of the wiser uses of time that I can imagine.

Let's examine this more deeply starting with the importance of high-performance breathing. The air we breathe is truly the source of life. The basic act of breathing is the thing that keeps us alive, from the first breath we take when we exit our mother's womb to our very last when it's time to leave our bodies behind.

This makes it the perfect 'physical' place to start now that we've discussed our mindset and relationships, and decided to put ourselves first and take responsibility for our health and wellness.

What actually happens when you breathe? While being so basic that we do it without even thinking, it's actually part of an incredibly sophisticated system at work in our bodies. Everyone will be familiar with the initial stages this system requires. First off, air is taken in through your nose and mouth when you inhale. From there, it travels down your airways to your lungs. As this happens, your diaphragm is contracting, increasing the size of your chest cavity, allowing your lungs to expand and suck the air in through your windpipe.

In the lungs, the air travels down bronchial tubes before entering air sacs, called alveoli. This is where your respiratory system filters out the oxygen required by your cells and delivers it into your bloodstream, with the help of the hemoglobin in your blood, in exchange for waste carbon dioxide pumped through the pulmonary artery.

It's this oxygen that fuels our brain and body. Carried by capillaries, it is taken to the pulmonary vein, whose job it is to send it straight to your heart. Your heart then pumps it around the body via your bloodstream, the oxygen escaping into your body's organs and tissues as it travels the blood vessels.

When you exhale, the chest cavity reduces in size, your diaphragm relaxes and air is forced up your airways then out your nose and mouth. This air carries out the waste carbon dioxide. It's a simple exchange playing on a continuous loop throughout our lives. On average, we will inhale and exhale 20,000 times a day.

So why, if this is what we do without thinking, am I saying we should treat it as an exercise and change the way we do it?

It all comes down to the important role oxygen plays in peak performance.

Peak Breathing Underpins Peak Performance

When the oxygen you've inhaled passes out of the blood vessels and into the cells of the surrounding tissue, it is converted into carbon dioxide and hydrogen oxide (i.e. water) in the cells' mitochondria. In the process, the oxygen enables the production of the molecule adenosine triphosphate (ATP) and the release of energy in our cells. This energy is the basis for every single function our bodies carry out – which makes oxygen the fuel our cells need to burn to carry out their jobs.

The better you are at bringing this vital oxygen into your body in an efficient way, in copious quantities, the better your body and brain will perform, in each and every function they undertake.

Just look at professional athletes. Breathing techniques are a focal component of their performance, whatever sport they compete in. In 2014, an article in The Wall Street explored why Olympic athletes were learning to hold their breath for over five minutes at a time.

A collection of athletes, including professional skiers, snowboarders and motocross riders attended a deep-dive camp as part of their training. It was all in aid of teaching them to control their breathing and remain relaxed under extreme circumstances so that they might excel in their sports.

Oxygenating the body means quicker thinking, quicker response times, quicker recovery – and less stress, when competing might mean you're putting your body under extra strain.

If you look at the founders of XPT Life, Gabrielle Rees, Laird Hamilton, Brian Mackenzie, Jenn Meredith Castillo and James Williams you'll find a collection of professional athletes and business people whose ability to perform at their peak is clear from their astonishing achievements. They attribute the practice of oxygenating breathing techniques with transformative powers and it lies at the center of their guidance for training for high performance.

My own high-performance breathing method is something I've tailored after learning techniques from a couple of different people. One was a personal development mentor and the other the Dutch daredevil Wim Hof, whose course I completed and loved.

This method of breathing, which I'll go on to describe in detail is something I can clearly associate with positive physical and mental results and everyone I've shared it with has enjoyed the same experience.

We've been through the theory; here are just some of the practical benefits you can tap into.

High-performance breathing:

- Helps your body relax by releasing tension.

- Helps relieve pain.

- Helps warm your body internally and protect it from the cold.

- Helps strengthen your cardiovascular system.

- Helps calm the mind and elevate your mood.

- Helps focus and concentration.

- Helps boost energy levels.

- Helps strengthen your immune system.

- Helps detoxify your body and release toxins.

- Helps improve the performance of your nervous system.

- Helps improve cellular regeneration and recovery.

What's a good way to practice breathing?

Breathe through your nose. Not only is it your airways' first natural line of defense, it also helps you breathe through your diaphragm.

Here are the different components of a high-performance breathing exercise I practice every morning and evening. Take the different steps that I do and see how you feel. Building high-performance breathing exercises into your daily routine is an important element of your High-Performance Plan.

Let's start off simple:

- Breathe in deeply through the nose.

- Inflate your navel area – not your chest area.

- Now breathe out through your nose or mouth while deflating your navel area.
  Do this 30-50 times

- On your last rep/breath, exhale deflating your naval area then hold your breath until you feel the need to breathe again.

- Take a deep breath through your nose and hold for ten seconds.

- Release your breath then repeat for 4-6 cycles

When I perform my high-performance breathing routine in its entirety, I repeat this sequence of steps 4 to 6 times after doing 30-50 breaths.

On the 5th or 6th round, I undertake the same cycle again, but this time when I exhale on my last breath, I do a set of push-ups with no oxygen. I then take a deep breath in, hold it for about ten seconds and exhale.

Deep Breathing Feeds Sexual Healing

This first high-performance breathing routine is something I follow, with exercises I've learned from Master Mantak Chia, a Taoist master who teaches people to reclaim their personal power through healing Taoist practices.

As Master Chia says in his foreword to Dennis Lewis's book, Natural Breathing, Natural

breathing is an integral part of the Tao… Through natural breathing we are able to support our overall health. We are able to improve the functioning and efficiency of our heart, lungs and other internal organs and systems. We are able to help balance our emotions. We are able to transform our stress and negativity into the energy that we can use for self-healing and self-development. And we are better able to extract and absorb the energy we need for spiritual growth and independence."

In a London Real interview, Master Chia explains the Eastern view of chi – your life force or bio electromagnetic power. When you're breathing, you're really drawing energy from the outside and channeling it inside.

He explains that there are five major organ sets to take care of:

The heart and small intestine.

The spleen, pancreas and stomach.

The lungs and large intestines.

The kidneys and bladder.

The liver and gall bladder.

Master Chia takes the viewer through several different breathing techniques to enable the fluid to flow within you, pointing out that, just like the earth, we're made up of seventy per cent water.

The better the fluid flows within you, the better the energy reaches every part of you. These simple exercises can be done in a sitting position, which I do each morning as part of my daily routine.

The first addresses the fluid in the spine and the brain:

Inhale, expanding your chest and expanding your stomach.

Raise your chin and elongate your neck.

Now exhale, curving your body down and inward. Bring your arms in with you.

Inhale again, stretching your body back out, raising your chin and elongating your neck. Raise your arms at your sides, bent at the elbows, opening your chest.

Exhale again, curving your body back down and inward.

Repeat this for several rounds. Feel the release of emotions on the exhale.

Now, rub your hands together to get them warm. This can be done sitting but standing is even better.

Place one hand at the back of your head, open palm cradling the cranium, the other at the base of your spine.

Rest and feel the warmth. Be conscious of the energy moving within you – that's when you're feeling the chi.

Focusing on your organs is the next step. Master Chia points to three areas:

Lower abdominal – where your sexual organs are situated and elimination occurs through the large intestine.

Middle abdominal – where your small intestine and kidneys are situated.

Upper abdominal – where the focus is digestion.

To exercise the lower abdominal area:

Place your hands over the area, flattening the stomach.

Inhale and exhale strongly through the nose, pushing the hands in and out in time.

Try to feel the organs squeezing.

To exercise the middle abdominal area:

Place your hands flat over the area.

Repeat the rounds of inhalation and exhalation through the nose, squeezing in.

Rest and rub the area warm.

Feel the energy flow.

To exercise the upper abdominal area:

Position your hands to the left and right of the area, fingers pointing inwards.

Repeat the series of strong breaths through the nose, drawing your hands in and pushing them out.

Massage the area with your hands, feeling the energy.

Heart and lungs are next:

Place your hands at your chest, over your ribcage.

Exhale, curving in your ribcage.

Inhale, expanding the chest. Feel the heart and lungs open.

Repeat 10 times, then rest.

Allow yourself to feel the love, joy and happiness.

Master Chia goes on to draw out the connection between sex and healing power and I want to pause here to give this its due, because I think when it comes to health and wellness, the power of sex can go unrecognized. I suppose the difference is that not everyone can start deciding to have sex the same way they can start deciding to sort out their breathing techniques or their eating habits but I really think it needs to be given its due as a natural part of life – and one that's seriously good for you!

Sex is tied to hormone regulation, which for both men and women can be integral when it comes to peak performance.

Indeed, it's important for living a happy and healthy life altogether! Now, I'm talking about sex as part of a healthy relationship here – in a healthy relationship, sex is usually present and hormone levels are at their optimum.

It's worth noting that in contrast, people who have lousy relationships usually have a lousy sex life and vice versa. Meanwhile, healthy people usually have better sex and unhealthy people struggle. If you don't believe me, check out the research. A common example is when you have a problem with your cardiovascular health; it usually means you have a problem with sexual performance.

Research has also found that high sexual drive is found in successful individuals. In Think and Grow Rich, Napoleon Hill devotes an entire chapter to the subject, saying that sex has "the possibility of three constructive potentialities." These are: the perpetuation of mankind; the maintenance of health; and the transformation of mediocrity into genius through transmutation. When it comes to the maintenance of health, he says, "As a therapeutic agency, it has no equal."

Overall, when it comes to sex and when it comes to the basics of breathing, the secret is focus and awareness. Focus on your breath with full awareness of what the process is doing for your body – and see the difference it makes. I actually consider the rounds of breathing I perform in the morning and at night a form of meditation, which is the subject of the next step.

The Practice and Art of Meditating

There are so many different ways that people practice meditation and meditation means different things to different people. Without a doubt, however, all those who practice it find it has a positive influence on their lives. The Buddhist Center describes it as a means of transforming the mind and I find that's exactly what it does.

Perhaps you already practice a form of meditation or maybe it's completely new to you; either way, it's an important practice with a host of beneficial effects. When it comes to performing at your peak, including meditation in your day in some form or another is a must!

The thing is, to practice it effectively, what you're doing isn't so important as **how** you're doing it. And it's all about awareness.

Whatever you're doing, you need to be doing it without distraction. Hence, when I'm practicing my breathing exercises I am, in fact, already meditating, just as, when I'm resting afterwards and listening to my Zen music, I'm meditating.

In the beginning, some people find it helpful to sit quietly and focus on just one thing, like a candle flame, for example. The aim is to clear the mind of all its chatter, emptying out all the warring thoughts and emotions and just be.

This means the opposite of the above holds true. Even when you're sitting down crossed-legged, in the lotus position, telling yourself you're meditating, if you let your busy mind intrude and you find yourself going over your to-do list in your head or bemoaning the things someone's done to annoy you this morning or considering the state the traffic's going to be in when you leave the house – then you're not actually meditating.

Putting the time aside isn't enough.

You need to train your mind, unlike when you're trying to learn a certain technique or adopt a set of positive affirmations, for example, you're not training your mind to take something on – you're training it to quiet itself. To calm itself. To empty itself.

But what is all this in aid of? What makes this a step towards peak performance?

A Walking Meditation

It helps if you do this alone and (it may go without saying) if you do this outside. It doesn't have to be a long walk or a strenuous hike. Just take ten minutes and see how you do. Just be aware that the more you practice it, the better you'll get at it!

Walk slowly and steadily; don't rush.

Now, focus on your feet.

Feel the sensation as each different part of your foot connects with the ground, from your heel through the arch to the ball of your foot and your toes.

Focus on that rolling motion, repeated as each foot is placed in front of the other.

If your mind drifts and you find yourself thinking about something else, bring your attention back to your feet, again and again.

Thank you for reading ...